50 Genetics Worksheets

Jeffry L. Shultz, Ph.D.

Other Titles by Dr. Shultz Available on Amazon

Genetics (Kindle Format)

X-Linked, Y-Linked and Mitochondrial Inheritance Pedigree Workbook

Autosomal Recessive Pedigree Workbook

SSR and SNP Molecular Marker Pedigree Workbook

300 Blank Pedigrees

500 Genetics Questions

Genetics Crossword and Word Search Puzzles

Genetics Lab Projects for an Academic Term (Student Edition)

Genetics Lab Projects for an Academic Term (Large Print Student Edition)

Genetics Lab Projects for an Academic Term (Instructors Edition)

Copyright © 2021 Jeffry L. Shultz
All rights reserved.
ISBN-13: 9798523989117

Cover art: Veil Nebula Supernova Remnant.
NASA Hubble Space Telescope, Public domain, via Wikimedia Commons.
https://commons.wikimedia.org/wiki/File:Veil_Nebula_Supernova_Remnant_(27993269556).jpg

Table of Contents

Using This Book — 3

Central Dogma
    How to Complete Sequence Conversion Worksheets — 5
    Sequence Conversion Worksheets — 6
    How to Complete Mutation Annotation Worksheets — 12
    Mutation Annotation Worksheets — 13
    How to Complete Probability of Random Match Worksheets — 15
    Random Match Worksheets — 16

Transmission Genetics
    How to Complete Cross Probability Worksheets — 19
    Cross Probability Worksheets — 20
    Pedigree Worksheets — 23
    How to Complete Forensics Worksheets — 30
    Forensics Worksheets — 32
    How to Complete Paternity Worksheets — 36
    Paternity Worksheets — 37

Population Genetics
    How to Complete Alleles in a Population Worksheets — 41
    Alleles in a Population Worksheets — 42

How to Complete Pull and Present Worksheets — 45
Pull and Present Worksheets — 46
Crossword Puzzles — 48
Lab-Based Exercises — 52
Matching Worksheets — 56
How to Complete Scientific Method Abstract Worksheets — 60
Scientific Method Abstract Worksheets — 61

Answers — 64

Using This Book

Disclaimer
This book was created as a supplemental learning/assessment resource: If you use this material for an exam, you must assume that within a short time the students at your institution will be aware of this book and *will have an answer key to your exam*.....

Educators
The questions in this book are organized by subject, then by type. The pages are formatted so that you can copy a single page and assign it as homework or in-class work. Each question is answered in the back of the book.

In many cases, a "How to complete" introduction is provided, unless the procedure for solving is obvious (like matching questions) or well beyond this book (several *different* pedigree inheritance types), in which case the instructor can use the answer key to derive a solution procedure.

Students
Use the table of contents to identify where the questions are located that you wish to study. Be aware that there are *substantial* differences in difficulty in the questions; Try a page of questions, then check the answers to make sure that you are on the right track.

How to Complete Sequence Conversion Worksheets

The sequence conversion worksheets illustrate the concept of co-linearity of gene expression - simply that the DNA directly leads to the polypeptide. mRNA and polypeptide molecules are read in a 5' direction. Only the template DNA is 3' to 5'. Copy this onto the back side of a sequence conversion worksheet ☺

Example…"Derive the missing mRNA strand. Indicate the 5' and 3' ends of your sequence, indicate the polypeptide from the start codon".

Polypeptide	__' - __ __ __ __ __ __ - __'
mRNA	__' - __ __ __ __ __ __ - __'
DNA Coding	__' - __ __ __ __ __ __ - __'
DNA Template	__' - A T A C T T A - __'

Step 1 - Derive the DNA Coding sequence, using complementary base pairing, Adenine (A) with Thymine (T) and Guanine (G) with Cytosine (C). Also enter the template direction.

Polypeptide	__' - __ __ __ __ __ __ - __'
mRNA	__' - __ __ __ __ __ __ - __'
DNA Coding	5' - T A T G A A T - 3'
DNA Template	3' - A T A C T T A - 5'

Step 2 - Derive the mRNA sequence by simply replacing the T's in the coding sequence with Uracil (U's) and enter the mRNA direction.

Polypeptide	__' - __ __ __ __ __ __ - __'
mRNA	5' - U A U G A A U - 3'
DNA Coding	5' - T A T G A A T - 3'
DNA Template	3' - A T A C T T A - 5'

Step 3 - Derive the polypeptide single letter code from the start codon (AUG) using the codon conversion below and enter the polypeptide direction.

Polypeptide	5' - M N - 3'
mRNA	5' - U <u>A U G</u> <u>A A U</u> - 3'
DNA Coding	5' - T A T G A A T - 3'
DNA Template	3' - A T A C T T A - 5'

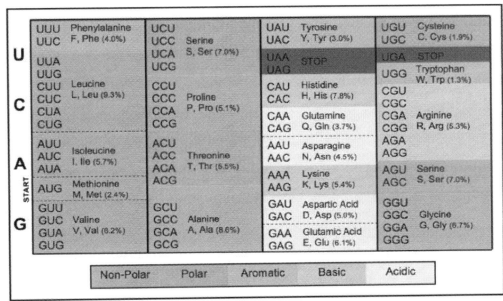

© J. L. Shultz

Sequence Conversion 1

Student: _____   Section/Course: _____

1. Derive the missing mRNA strand. Indicate the 5' and 3' ends of your sequence
   mRNA   __'- __ __ __ __ __ __ -__'
   DNA Coding   __'- G C T C A T G -__'

2. Derive the missing Coding strand. Indicate the 5' and 3' ends of your sequence
   DNA Coding   __'- __ __ __ __ __ __ -__'
   DNA Template __'- A T G C T C A -__'

3. Derive the missing mRNA strand. Indicate the 5' and 3' ends of your sequence
   mRNA   __'- __ __ __ __ __ __ -__'
   DNA Coding   __'- __ __ __ __ __ __ -__'
   DNA Template __'- A T C C A C A -__'

4. Derive the missing Coding strand. Indicate the 5' and 3' ends of your sequence
   DNA Coding   __'- __ __ __ __ __ __ -__'
   DNA Template __'- C T T C G C T -__'

5. Derive the missing Template strand. Indicate the 5' and 3' ends of your sequence
   mRNA   __'- U C G U C G U -__'
   DNA Coding   __'- __ __ __ __ __ __ -__'
   DNA Template __'- __ __ __ __ __ __ -__'

6. Derive the missing mRNA strand. Indicate the 5' and 3' ends of your sequence
   mRNA   __'- __ __ __ __ __ __ -__'
   DNA Coding   __'- __ __ __ __ __ __ -__'
   DNA Template __'- A T G G T T A -__'

7. Derive the missing Coding strand. Indicate the 5' and 3' ends of your sequence
   DNA Coding   __'- __ __ __ __ __ __ -__'
   DNA Template __'- C T T G C T A -__'

8. Derive the missing Template strand. Indicate the 5' and 3' ends of your sequence
   DNA Coding   __'- T G C A A T C -__'
   DNA Template __'- __ __ __ __ __ __ -__'

9. Derive the missing mRNA strand. Indicate the 5' and 3' ends of your sequence
   mRNA   __'- __ __ __ __ __ __ -__'
   DNA Coding   __'- __ __ __ __ __ __ -__'
   DNA Template __'- A A C G T A G -__'

10. Derive the missing Template strand. Indicate the 5' and 3' ends of your sequence
    mRNA   __'- U C A U A G C -__'
    DNA Coding   __'- __ __ __ __ __ __ -__'
    DNA Template __'- __ __ __ __ __ __ -__'

Sequence Conversion 2   Student: _____   Section/Course: _____

1. Derive the missing Template strand. Indicate the 5' and 3' ends of your sequence
   DNA Coding   __'- G C C T C G A -__'
   DNA Template   __'- __ __ __ __ __ __ __ -__'

2. Derive the missing Coding strand. Indicate the 5' and 3' ends of your sequence
   mRNA   __'- U C U A G C G -__'
   DNA Coding   __'- __ __ __ __ __ __ __ -__'

3. Derive the missing mRNA strand. Indicate the 5' and 3' ends of your sequence
   mRNA   __'- __ __ __ __ __ __ __ -__'
   DNA Coding   __'- __ __ __ __ __ __ __ -__'
   DNA Template   __'- G C T A T G G -__'

4. Derive the missing Template strand. Indicate the 5' and 3' ends of your sequence
   mRNA   __'- U U C G C A U -__'
   DNA Coding   __'- __ __ __ __ __ __ __ -__'
   DNA Template   __'- __ __ __ __ __ __ __ -__'

5. Derive the missing mRNA strand. Indicate the 5' and 3' ends of your sequence
   mRNA   __'- __ __ __ __ __ __ __ -__'
   DNA Coding   __'- __ __ __ __ __ __ __ -__'
   DNA Template   __'- A T T C A T G -__'

6. Derive the missing Template strand. Indicate the 5' and 3' ends of your sequence
   DNA Coding   __'- T C A C T G C -__'
   DNA Template   __'- __ __ __ __ __ __ __ -__'

7. Derive the missing single letter polypeptide sequence from the start codon. Indicate the 5' and 3' ends.
   Polypeptide   __'-   -__'
   mRNA   __' - AUCUGAUGACC - __'

8. Derive the missing single letter polypeptide sequence from the start codon. Indicate the 5' and 3' ends.
   Polypeptide   __'-   -__'
   mRNA   __' - UCAUGUCCGCA - __'

9. Derive the missing single letter polypeptide sequence from the start codon. Indicate the 5' and 3' ends.
   Polypeptide   __'-   -__'
   mRNA   __'- __ __ __ __ __ __ __ __ __ __ -__'
   DNA Coding   __'- T A T G C G A C T G C -__'

10. Derive the missing single letter polypeptide sequence from the start codon. Indicate the 5' and 3' ends.
    Polypeptide   __'-   -__'
    mRNA   __'- __ __ __ __ __ __ __ __ __ __ -__'
    DNA Coding   __'- __ __ __ __ __ __ __ __ __ __ -__'
    DNA Template   __'- G T A C A C G T C G A -__'

Sequence Conversion 3   Student: _____   Section/Course: _____

1. The genomic sequence of a gene is 10,000 bp long, the edited mRNA is 3,000 bp long and _____ the polypeptide is 930 amino acids long. How many codons are in the edited mRNA?
   - A   2,790
   - B   930
   - C   310
   - D   6
   - E   Unable to determine

2. Derive the missing mRNA strand. Indicate the 5' and 3' ends of your sequence
   mRNA   __' - __ __ __ __ __ __ - __'
   DNA Coding   __' - T C T C G T G - __'

3. Derive the missing Template strand. Indicate the 5' and 3' ends of your sequence
   mRNA   __' - U C G G C G U - __'
   DNA Coding   __' - __ __ __ __ __ __ - __'
   DNA Template   __' - __ __ __ __ __ __ - __'

4. Derive the missing Coding strand. Indicate the 5' and 3' ends of your sequence
   DNA Coding   __' - __ __ __ __ __ __ - __'
   DNA Template   __' - C T T G C G A - __'

5. Derive the missing mRNA strand. Indicate the 5' and 3' ends of your sequence
   mRNA   __' - __ __ __ __ __ __ - __'
   DNA Coding   __' - __ __ __ __ __ __ - __'
   DNA Template   __' - G A T G T A G - __'

6. Derive the missing Template strand. Indicate the 5' and 3' ends of your sequence
   DNA Coding   __' - G C C T C G A - __'
   DNA Template   __' - __ __ __ __ __ __ - __'

7. Derive the missing mRNA strand. Indicate the 5' and 3' ends of your sequence
   mRNA   __' - __ __ __ __ __ __ - __'
   DNA Coding   __' - __ __ __ __ __ __ - __'
   DNA Template   __' - G C T G T G G - __'

8. Derive the missing mRNA strand. Indicate the 5' and 3' ends of your sequence
   mRNA   __' - __ __ __ __ __ __ - __'
   DNA Coding   __' - __ __ __ __ __ __ - __'
   DNA Template   __' - A T T T A T G - __'

9. Derive the missing single letter polypeptide sequence from the start codon. Indicate the 5' and 3' ends.
   Polypeptide   __' - __ __ __ __ __ __ - __'
   mRNA   __' - AGCUGAUGACC - __'

10. Derive the missing single letter polypeptide sequence from the start codon. Indicate the 5' and 3' ends.
    Polypeptide   __' - __ __ __ __ __ __ - __'
    mRNA   __' - __ __ __ __ __ __ __ __ __ - __'
    DNA Coding   __' - T A T G T G G C T G C - __'

Sequence Conversion 4   Student: _____   Section/Course: _____

1. The genomic sequence of a gene is 10,000 bp long, the edited mRNA is 3,000 bp long and the polypeptide is 930 amino acids long. How many base pairs are in genes' codons?
   - A 2,790
   - B 930
   - C 310
   - D 6
   - E Unable to determine

2. Derive the missing Coding strand. Indicate the 5' and 3' ends of your sequence
   DNA Coding   __'- __ __ __ __ __ __ -__'
   DNA Template   __'- G T T C T C A -__'

3. Derive the missing Coding strand. Indicate the 5' and 3' ends of your sequence
   DNA Coding   __'- __ __ __ __ __ __ -__'
   DNA Template   __'- C T T C G C T -__'

4. Derive the missing mRNA strand. Indicate the 5' and 3' ends of your sequence
   mRNA   __'- __ __ __ __ __ __ -__'
   DNA Coding   __'- __ __ __ __ __ __ -__'
   DNA Template   __'- G T T G T T A -__'

5. Derive the missing Template strand. Indicate the 5' and 3' ends of your sequence
   mRNA   __'- G C G G A U C -__'
   DNA Coding   __'- __ __ __ __ __ __ -__'
   DNA Template   __'- __ __ __ __ __ __ -__'

6. Derive the missing Coding strand. Indicate the 5' and 3' ends of your sequence
   mRNA   __'- U C G A G C G -__'
   DNA Coding   __'- __ __ __ __ __ __ -__'

7. Derive the missing Template strand. Indicate the 5' and 3' ends of your sequence
   mRNA   __'- G U C G G A U -__'
   DNA Coding   __'- __ __ __ __ __ __ -__'
   DNA Template   __'- __ __ __ __ __ __ -__'

8. Derive the missing Template strand. Indicate the 5' and 3' ends of your sequence
   DNA Coding   __'- T C T C G G C -__'
   DNA Template   __'- __ __ __ __ __ __ -__'

9. Derive the missing single letter polypeptide sequence from the start codon. Indicate the 5' and 3' ends.
   Polypeptide   __'- __ __ __ __ -__'
   mRNA   __'- UCAUGUCCGGA -__'

10. Derive the missing single letter polypeptide sequence from the start codon. Indicate the 5' and 3' ends.
    Polypeptide   __'- __ __ __ __ -__'
    mRNA   __'- __ __ __ __ __ __ __ __ __ __ -__'
    DNA Coding   __'- __ __ __ __ __ __ __ __ __ __ -__'
    DNA Template   __'- G T G T A C G T G G A -__'

Sequence Conversion 5   Student: _____   Section/Course: _____

1. The genomic sequence of a gene is 10,000 bp long, the edited mRNA is 3,000 bp long and the polypeptide is 310 amino acids long. How many codons are in the edited mRNA?
   - A 2,790
   - B 930
   - C 310
   - D 6
   - E Unable to determine

2. Derive the missing Template strand. Indicate the 5' and 3' ends of your sequence
   - DNA Coding   __'- T G C T G T C -__'
   - DNA Template   __'- _ _ _ _ _ _ _ -__'

3. Derive the missing mRNA strand. Indicate the 5' and 3' ends of your sequence
   - mRNA   __'- _ _ _ _ _ _ _ -__'
   - DNA Coding   __'- G A T A C T G -__'

4. Derive the missing Coding strand. Indicate the 5' and 3' ends of your sequence
   - DNA Coding   __'- _ _ _ _ _ _ -__'
   - DNA Template   __'- G A T T A C A -__'

5. Derive the missing mRNA strand. Indicate the 5' and 3' ends of your sequence
   - mRNA   __'- _ _ _ _ _ _ -__'
   - DNA Coding   __'- _ _ _ _ _ _ -__'
   - DNA Template   __'- A T C G T C A -__'

6. Derive the missing Template strand. Indicate the 5' and 3' ends of your sequence
   - mRNA   __'- U G G A C A U -__'
   - DNA Coding   __'- _ _ _ _ _ _ -__'
   - DNA Template   __'- _ _ _ _ _ _ -__'

7. Derive the missing Coding strand. Indicate the 5' and 3' ends of your sequence
   - DNA Coding   __'- _ _ _ _ _ _ -__'
   - DNA Template   __'- C C T A C G A -__'

8. Derive the missing single letter polypeptide sequence from the start codon. Indicate the 5' and 3' ends.
   - Polypeptide   __'- _____ -__'
   - mRNA   __'- AUAUGAGGCCC -__'

9. Derive the missing single letter polypeptide sequence from the start codon. Indicate the 5' and 3' ends.
   - Polypeptide   __'- _____ -__'
   - mRNA   __'- GCAUGUCCCCA -__'

10. Derive the missing single letter polypeptide sequence from the start codon. Indicate the 5' and 3' ends.
    - Polypeptide   __'- _____ -__'
    - mRNA   __'- _ _ _ _ _ _ _ _ _ _ -__'
    - DNA Coding   __'- T T C G C C T C C G A -__'

Sequence Conversion 6

1. Derive the missing mRNA strand.
- mRNA: 5'-AAGGUGU-3'
- DNA Coding: 5'-AAGGTGT-3'
- DNA Template: 3'-TTCCACA-5'

2. Derive the missing Template strand.
- mRNA: 5'-UCUUCGU-3'
- DNA Coding: 5'-TCTTCGT-3'
- DNA Template: 3'-AGAAGCA-5'

3. Derive the missing Template strand.
- DNA Coding: 5'-TGCAATC-3'
- DNA Template: 3'-ACGTTAG-5'

4. Derive the missing mRNA strand.
- mRNA: 5'-UUACAUC-3'
- DNA Coding: 5'-TTACATC-3'
- DNA Template: 3'-AATGTAG-5'

5. Derive the missing Template strand.
- mRNA: 5'-UUCUCAU-3'
- DNA Coding: 5'-TTCTCAT-3'
- DNA Template: 3'-AAGAGTA-5'

6. Derive the missing Template strand.
- DNA Coding: 5'-TCATTGC-3'
- DNA Template: 3'-AGTAACG-5'

7. Derive the missing polypeptide.
- Polypeptide: N'-M-C' (Met, then stop codon UGA)
- mRNA: 5'-AUGUGAUUACC-3'

8. Derive the missing polypeptide.
- Polypeptide: N'-M-C-A-C' (Met-Cys-Ala)
- mRNA: 5'-UAAUGUGCGCA-3'

9. Derive the missing polypeptide.
- Polypeptide: N'-M-R-C' (Met-Arg, then stop codon UAG)
- mRNA: 5'-UAUGAGGUAGC-3'
- DNA Coding: 5'-TATGAGGTAGC-3'

10. Derive the missing TEMPLATE sequence.
- Polypeptide: N'-M-T-G-C'
- mRNA: 5'-AUG ACC GGC-3'
- DNA Coding: 5'-ATG ACC GGC-3'
- DNA Template: 3'-TAC TGG CCG-5'

Information Needed to Complete Mutation Annotation Worksheets

The mutation annotation worksheets illustrate the accurate annotation of change in a sequence. There are several ways this annotation can occur in literature, so try not to get too worried about the *exact* way that the annotation is presented - try instead to understand what it is attempting to convey. Copy this onto the back side of the mutation annotation worksheet ☺.

Terminology Used to Describe Mutations

c. annotation indicates a change in the DNA coding sequence
p. annotation indicates a change in the polypeptide sequence. *ONLY applies to mRNA (EXON) sequences*
Wild type is the allele most common in a specific population.
Mutant is a rare allele in the specific population.
Reversion is the change of a mutant allele back to the wild-type.
Deleterious mutation decreases chances of survival and reproduction.
Beneficial mutation enhances survival or reproduction.
Conditional mutations affect the phenotype only under certain conditions.
Neutral mutation is a missense mutation that replaces an amino acid for another with similar chemistry or that have no effect on the function of the subsequent polypeptide.
Lethal mutation results in death of the organism.

Silent mutations do not change the amino acid incorporated into the polypeptide.
May not be totally silent, as the mutation may affect regulation of the gene via siRNA or microRNA.
c.68T>C (p.(=))   NOT p.Ala22Ala. *All silent mutations should be annotated at the DNA level.*

Mis-sense mutations change the amino acid incorporated in one position of the polypeptide.
p.Leu4356Pro   Leucine at position 4356 changed to proline.

Non-sense mutations create a new stop codon at the mutation point.
p.Ser1326*   Indicates a serine has been changed to a stop codon.

Frameshift mutations change the reading frame, leading to a stop codon.
p.Leu146fs   Frame shift mutation in the polypeptide at the Leucine at 146 bp. (short form).
    This mutation will result in premature termination of translation.
p.Leu146Phe*fs7   Frame shift mutation in the polypeptide at the Leucine at 146 bp. (long form).
    The new amino acid is a phenylalanine, followed by a stop seven codons later.

U	UUU UUC	Phenylalanine F, Phe (4.0%)	UCU UCC UCA UCG	Serine S, Ser (7.0%)	UAU UAC	Tyrosine Y, Tyr (3.0%)	UGU UGC	Cysteine C, Cys (1.9%)
	UUA UUG				UAA UAG	STOP	UGA	STOP
							UGG	Tryptophan W, Trp (1.3%)
C	CUU CUC CUA CUG	Leucine L, Leu (9.3%)	CCU CCC CCA CCG	Proline P, Pro (5.1%)	CAU CAC	Histidine H, His (7.8%)	CGU CGC CGA CGG	Arginine R, Arg (5.3%)
					CAA CAG	Glutamine Q, Gln (3.7%)		
A	AUU AUC AUA	Isoleucine I, Ile (5.7%)	ACU ACC ACA ACG	Threonine T, Thr (5.5%)	AAU AAC	Asparagine N, Asn (4.5%)	AGA AGG	
	AUG (START)	Methionine M, Met (2.4%)			AAA AAG	Lysine K, Lys (5.4%)	AGU AGC	Serine S, Ser (7.0%)
G	GUU GUC GUA GUG	Valine V, Val (6.2%)	GCU GCC GCA GCG	Alanine A, Ala (8.6%)	GAU GAC	Aspartic Acid D, Asp (5.0%)	GGU GGC GGA GGG	Glycine G, Gly (6.7%)
					GAA GAG	Glutamic Acid E, Glu (6.1%)		

Non-Polar   Polar   Aromatic   Basic   Acidic

© J. L. Shultz

Mutation Annotation 1   Student: _____   Section/Course:_____

1. ___ The mutation annotation p.Leu231Thr indicates what?
   - A   The coding sequence at DNA bp 231 has been changed to a Threonine
   - B   The amino sequence at DNA bp 231 has been changed to a Threonine in a sequence
   - C   The amino acid at position 231 has been changed to a threonine in a polypeptide
   - D   The amino acid at position 231 has been changed to a stop codon in a polypeptide

2. ___ Which of the following sequences would result from the annotation c.1026dupGA[3]?
   THINK CAREFULLY!
   - A   5' …AUCACGAUAGAUACAGAUA..3'
   - B   5' …ATCACTATACAGATA..3'
   - C   3' …ATCCTCTCTGCTACAGATA..5'
   - D   5' …ATCACTAATAATAACAGATA..3'
   - E   5' …ATCACTAUATTACAGAUA..3'

3. ___ Which of the following sequences would result from the annotation c.72dupCAG[4]?
   THINK CAREFULLY!
   - A   5' …AUCACUAUAUAUACAGAUA..3'
   - B   5' …ATCACTATACAGATA..3'
   - C   3' …ATCACTATACAGATA..5'
   - D   5' …ATCACTAATAATAACAGATA..3'
   - E   3' …ATCAGTCGTCGTCGTCAUA..5'

4. What is the sequence that would result from the mutation c.4G>C?
   Wild-type   5'- T A T G A G G T A G C -3'
   After Mutation   5'- __ __ __ __ __ __ __ __ __ __ __ -3'

5. What is the sequence that would result from the mutation p.M6V?
   Wild-type   5'- L A T R A M G S Q G W -3'
   After Mutation   5'- __ __ __ __ __ __ __ __ __ __ __ -3'

6. What single base change would cause the mutation in question 5?

7. Indicate the mutation c.18T>A in the following sequence
   Sequence after Mutation   5' - ATCACATGAGTAGCAGTAAGTAGGATCAGTACAG - 3'

8. Indicate the mutation c.12Adel in the following sequence
   Sequence after Mutation   5' - ATCACATGAGTAGCAGTAAGTAGGATCAGTACAG - 3'

9. Indicate the mutation p.Gln3His*fs3 in the following sequence (You will need to convert this sequence to a polypeptide to get your answer…)
   Sequence after Mutation   5' - ATCACATGAGTCATAGTAAGTAGGATCAGTACAG - 3'

10. Question 9 indicates a change from Glutamine to Histidine, which bp of the Glutamine codon was deleted and which bp replaced it?

Mutation Annotation 2   Student: _____   Section/Course: _____

1. ___ Which of the following mutations is the most problematic for an organism?
    - A   2 bp deletion in an intron
    - B   3 bp deletion in an exon
    - C   1 bp insertion in an exon
    - D   6 bp deletion in an intron
    - E   Unable to determine

2. ___ Which of the following mutations is the least problematic for an organism (multiple answers possible)?
    - A   2 bp deletion in an intron
    - B   3 bp deletion in an exon
    - C   1 bp insertion in an exon
    - D   6 bp deletion in an intron
    - E   Unable to determine

3. ___ Which of the following mutations is the most problematic for gene A (3,846 amino acids long)?
    - A   2 bp deletion in an intron
    - B   2 bp deletion in the 236th exon
    - C   1 bp insertion in the 3834th exon
    - D   6 bp deletion in an intron
    - E   Unable to determine

4. ___ Which of the following mutations is the most problematic for an organism?
    - A   p.R146G
    - B   c.R146G
    - C   p.1384C>T
    - D   c.1384C>T
    - E   Either A or D

5. What is the sequence that would result from the mutation c.7G>T?
    Wild-type   5' - T A T G A G G T A G C - 3'
    After Mutation   5' - __ __ __ __ __ __ __ __ __ __ __ - 3'

6. What is the sequence that would result from the mutation p.W11C?
    Wild-type   5' - L A T R A M G S Q G W - 3'
    After Mutation   5' - __ __ __ __ __ __ __ __ __ __ __ - 3'

7. What single base change would cause the mutation in question 6?

8. Indicate the mutation c.7C>A in the following sequence
    Sequence after Mutation   5' - ATCACAAGAGTAGCAGTAAGTAGGATCAGTACAG - 3'

9. Indicate the mutation p.Glu7Term in the following sequence (You will need to convert this sequence to a polypeptide to get your answer…)
    Sequence after Mutation   5' - ATCACATGAGTCATAGTAAGTATTAACAGTACAG - 3'

10. Question 9 indicates a change from Glutamic Acid to a termination codon, which bp of the Glutamic Acid codon was mutated and which bp replaced it?

How to Complete Probability of Random Match Worksheets

When working with DNA, it is useful to know how "specific" a fragment of sequence is. To start out simply, think of how likely you will encounter an Adenine (A) in a sequence - assuming an equal and random distribution of base pairs, you should encounter this *every 4 base pairs* meaning that at each bp position, there is a ¼ chance of a specific base pair. If you have a 5 bp sequence like *5'-ATAGC-3'* it should occur once every 1,024 bp or, ¼ x ¼ x ¼ x ¼ x ¼ = 1/1,024.

A general rule of thumb is three 0's for every five base pairs; Thus a 20 bp fragment has about 1 in 1,000,000,000,000 (trillion) chance that a random match will be found to your sequence. To verify this really high number, try entering 4^{20} in your calculator; you will get something like 1.099×10^{12}.

Why is this important? Knowing how to calculate the specificity of a sequence is useful in PCR primer design and in selection of an appropriate restriction enzyme or primer length to use.

PCR Primers

The PCR process is essentially a genetic copy machine and by supplying the proper components, millions of copies of the target DNA sequence can be created in a matter of hours. Primers are short sequences of DNA that start the PCR reaction at a place in the genome, based on their sequence. For instance, Randomly Amplified Polymorphic DNA or "RAPD" primers were used in the 1990's and early 2000's to amplify fragments of DNA in large genomes. These primers were 10 bp long and randomly annealed to the target DNA about every 1 million base pairs - that may sound specific, but in the 3 *billion* bp Human genome, these primers would find a match nearly *3,000 times*, making them less than specific and hard to reproduce. They were rapidly (pun intended!) replaced by microsatellite markers (still used by the FBI in their CODIS database and for paternity testing by private companies) which are about 20bp long and are specific to 1 in 1 trillion bp - it is kind of amazing how much of a difference 10 base pairs can make!

Restriction Enzymes are molecular enzymes that cut a fragment of DNA based on a specific sequence (usually 4-8 bp in length), with most being endonucleases - which recognize a sequence *within* a molecule and cut accordingly. Because of this short length, these are usually used on small genomes such as Lambda, which is only about 48,000 bp long.

The restriction enzyme HaeIII *cuts the specific site 5'-...GGCC... -3'*, leaving the following DNA sequences:

```
5'-......GG|CC...... -3'        5'-......GG    CC...... -3'
3'-......CC|GG...... -5'        3'-......CC    GG...... -5'
```

The restriction enzyme HindIII is a different enzyme which *cuts the specific site 5'-AAGCTT -3'*, as below

```
5'-......A|AGCTT...... -3'   →   5'-......A        AGCTT...... -3'
3'-......TTCGA|A...... -5'        3'-......TTCGA        A...... -5'
```

How often will these restriction enzymes cleave random DNA? HaeIII *recognizes* "GGCC", a four base cutter, or ¼ x ¼ x ¼ x ¼ = 1/256 or once every 256 bp of random DNA. HindIII recognizes "AAGCTT", a six base cutter, or ¼ x ¼ x ¼ x ¼ x ¼ x ¼ = 1/4,096 or once every 4,096 bp of random DNA.

OK, now try to solve some of these progressively harder probability problems….

Probability of Random Match 1 Student: _____ Section/Course: _____

1. Calculate the odds (in fractions) of encountering the sequence 5' - ATACGA - 3' in a random fragment of DNA.

2. Calculate the odds (in fractions) of encountering the sequence 5' - GGCC - 3' in a random fragment of DNA.

3. Calculate the odds (in fractions) of encountering the sequence 5' - TTTTA - 3' in a random fragment of DNA.

4. The HindIII enzyme recognizes the following sequence 5'-AAGCTT -3'. Approximately how many times will it cut a random DNA sequence of 100,000 bp?
   - A 4
   - B 6
   - C 12
   - D 25
   - E None of the above

5. The HaeIII enzyme recognizes the following sequence 5'-GGCC -3'. Approximately how many times will it cut a random DNA sequence of 1,000 bp?
   - A 4
   - B 6
   - C 12
   - D 25
   - E None of the above

6. What is the sequence recognized by BamHI?

7. You have a 1 million bp fragment of DNA that you wish to cut into about fourteen fragments - what size of restriction site will your restriction enzyme need to recognize?

8. How many times would you expect to find a 15 bp primer sequence in Humans (3 Bbp DNA)

9. After performing PCR on a Human sample, your product looks smeared when run on an agarose gel. What could be wrong with the primers (more than one answer may be correct)?
   - A They are too specific (long)
   - B They are not designed for Human
   - C The annealing temperature was too low
   - D They were not put in the reaction
   - E They are too short

10. You cut a 100,000 bp fragment of DNA with XhoI, how many fragments will likely result?

Probability of Random Match 2   Student: _____   Section/Course:_____

1. Calculate the odds (in fractions) of encountering the sequence 5' - ATACTGA - 3' in a random fragment of DNA.

2. Calculate the odds (in fractions) of encountering the sequence 5' - ATG - 3' in a random fragment of DNA.

3. Calculate the odds (in fractions) of encountering the sequence 5' - TACAGTAC - 3' in a random fragment of DNA.

4. The EcoRI enzyme recognizes the following sequence 5'-GAATTC -3'. Approximately how many times will it cut a random DNA sequence of 10,000 bp?
   A   4   D   2
   B   6   E   None of the above
   C   12

5. The BamHI enzyme recognizes the following sequence 5' - GGATCC - 3'. Approximately how many times will it cut a random DNA sequence of 1,000,000 bp?
   A   4   D   25
   B   250   E   None of the above
   C   12

6. What is the sequence recognized by SmaI?

7. You have a 100,000 bp fragment of DNA that you wish to cut, how often will SmaI cut this DNA?

8. How many times would you expect to find a 10 bp primer sequence in Humans (3 Bbp DNA)

9. After performing PCR on a Human sample, your bands look sharp when run on an agarose gel. What worked with the primers (more than one answer may be correct)?
   A   They were specific   D   They were not put in the reaction
   B   They were designed for Human   E   They ran out after the second cycle
   C   The annealing temperature was too low

10. You cut a 1,000,000 bp fragment of DNA with Bsp13I, how many fragments will likely result?

Probability of Random Match 3   Student: _____   Section/Course: _____
(Challenge Questions)

1. Calculate the odds (in fractions) of encountering the sequence 5' - ATACGA - 3' in a random fragment of DNA with a 40% G/C content.

2. Calculate the odds (in fractions) of encountering the sequence 5' - GGCC - 3' in a random fragment of DNA with a 60% G/C content.

3. Calculate the odds (in fractions) of encountering the sequence encoding the *polypeptide* 5' - PQW - 3' in a random fragment of DNA.

4. The *Hind*III enzyme recognizes the following sequence 5'-AAGCTT -3'. Approximately how many times will it cut a random DNA sequence of 100,000 bp?
   - A   4
   - B   6
   - C   12
   - D   25
   - E   None of the above

5. The *Hae*III enzyme recognizes the following sequence 5'- GGCC -3'. Approximately how many times will it cut a random DNA sequence of 10,000 bp?
   - A   4
   - B   40
   - C   12
   - D   25
   - E   None of the above

6. What is the sequence recognized by HaeII?

7. How many restriction sites will HaeII find in a 100,000 bp fragment of DNA?

8. How many times would you expect to find a 16 bp primer sequence in Humans (3 Bbp DNA)

9. After performing PCR on a prokaryote sample, your product looks smeared when run on an agarose gel. What could be wrong with the primers (more than one answer may be correct)?
   - A   They are too specific (long)
   - B   They are not designed for prokaryotes
   - C   The annealing temperature was too low
   - D   They were not put in the reaction
   - E   They are too short

10. You cut a 100,000 bp fragment of DNA with MroI, how many fragments will likely result?

How to Complete Cross Probability Worksheets

When calculating the probability of a cross that involves several genes, several methods can be used. First a di-hybrid Punnett square can be used for two genes, each with two segregating alleles. Second, a Tri-hybrid forked line diagram may also be used for a cross involving three genes and two alleles. I was taught to use these tools when I went to school, and in over twenty years I have never *actually* used them. The following method for calculating a resulting genotype is based on a simple Punnett square.

The answer to a simple cross of one gene and two alleles is given by the following "Y" gene example.

Question: Mendel crossed homozygous parents with Yellow (YY) and green (yy) seed to make yellow F_1 seed. These F_1 seed were then selfed. What percent of seed in the F_2 generation will be yellow?

Step 1: Draw a Punnett square, adding the F_1 alleles and the progeny genotypes.

	Y	y
Y	YY	Yy
y	Yy	yy

Step 2: Because capital "Y" indicates that the yellow allele is dominant (and the F_1 seed is also yellow, which *proves* the yellow allele is dominant), any genotype with at least one "Y" allele will be yellow. Thus the shaded squares indicate yellow seed and the answer to this question - 75%.

	Y	y
Y	**YY**	**Yy**
y	**Yy**	yy

The answer to a more complex cross of two or more genes, each with two alleles is given by the following example.

*Question: In a cross between parent 1 AaBBcc x Parent 2 AaBbCc, what is the chance in fractions of having the genotype **aaBbCc** in the progeny?*

Simply multiply the probability of each genotype from the parental genotypes to arrive at the fraction %

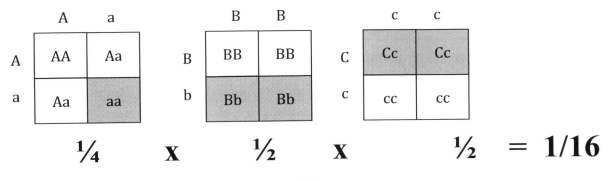

Cross Probability 1   Student: _____   Section/Course: _____

1. Mendel crossed homozygous parents with Yellow (YY) and green (yy) seed to make yellow F_1 seed. These F_1 seed were then selfed. What is the percentage of seed in the F_2 generation that will be homozygous yellow?

2. Mendel crossed homozygous parents with Yellow (YY) and green (yy) seed to make yellow F_1 seed. These F_1 seed were then selfed. What is the percentage of seed in the F_2 generation that will be heterozygous green?

3. Mendel crossed homozygous parents with Yellow (YY) and green (yy) seed to make yellow F_1 seed. These F_1 seed were then selfed. What is the percentage of seed in the F_2 generation that will be homozygous green?

4. Mendel crossed homozygous parents with Yellow (YY) and green (yy) seed to make yellow F_1 seed. These F_1 seed were then selfed. What is the percentage of seed in the F_1 generation that were heterozygous yellow?

5. Mendel crossed homozygous parents with Yellow (YY) and green (yy) seed to make yellow F_1 seed. These F_1 seed were then selfed. What is the probability (in fractions) that an F_2 seed chosen at random **from among the yellow seeds** will breed true (produce only one phenotype) when selfed?

6. In a cross between parent 1 AaBbCc x Parent 2 AaBbCc, what is the chance in fractions of a progeny having the genotype AaBbCc?

7. In a cross between parent 1 AaBbCc x Parent 2 AaBbCc, what is the chance in fractions of a progeny having the genotype AABbCC?

8. In a cross between parent 1 AaBbCc x Parent 2 AaBbCc, what is the chance in fractions of having a progenythe genotype aaBbCc?

9. Two healthy parents have nine healthy children, but their tenth child exhibits severe mental and physical issues. What is the most likely cause?
    Chromosome 21 non-disjunction

10. Two related, healthy parents have two healthy children, but their third child exhibits severe mental and physical issues. What is the most likely cause?
    Autosomal Recessive disease

Cross Probability 2   Student: _____ Section/Course: _____

1. Mendel crossed homozygous parents with Yellow (YY) and green (yy) seed to make yellow F_1 seed. These F_1 seed were then selfed. What is the percentage of seed in the F_2 generation that will be heterozygous yellow?

2. Mendel crossed homozygous parents with Yellow (YY) and green (yy) seed to make yellow F_1 seed. These F_1 seed were then selfed. What is the percentage of seed in the F_1 generation that were homozygous yellow?

3. Mendel crossed homozygous parents with Yellow (YY) and green (yy) seed to make yellow F_1 seed. These F_1 seed were then selfed. What is the percentage of seed in the F_1 generation that were heterozygous yellow?

4. Mendel crossed homozygous parents with Yellow (YY) and green (yy) seed to make yellow F_1 seed. These F_1 seed were then selfed. What is the probability (in fractions) that an F_2 seed chosen at random **from among the yellow seeds** will breed true (produce only one phenotype) when selfed?

5. Mendel crossed homozygous parents with Yellow (YY) and green (yy) seed to make yellow F_1 seed. These F_1 seed were then selfed. What is the probability (in fractions) that an F_2 seed chosen at random **from among the green seeds** will breed true (produce only one phenotype) when selfed?

6. In a cross between parent 1 AaBbCc x Parent 2 AaBbCc, what is the chance in fractions of a progeny having the genotype AaBbCc?

7. In a cross between parent 1 AaBbCc x Parent 2 AaBbCc, what is the chance in fractions of a progeny having the genotype AABbCC?

8. In a cross between parent 1 AaBbCc x Parent 2 AaBbCc, what is the chance in fractions of having the genotype aaBbCc?

9. In a cross between parent 1 AaBbCc x Parent 2 AaBbCc, what is the chance in fractions of having the genotype AaBbCc?

10. A couple is concerned that a rare x-linked recessive disease occurs in the mothers family. Tests confirm that a SNP that causes this disease. If they have a child, what is the chance they will *not* be a carrier or affected?

Cross Probability 3
Challenge Questions

Student: _____ Section/Course: _____

1. You cross homozygous pea plants with Tall (TT) and short (tt) height to make F_1 plants that are *taller than either of the parents*. These F_1 plants were then selfed. What is the percentage of progeny in the F_2 generation that are taller than either P_1 parent?

2. You cross homozygous pea plants with Tall (TT) and short (tt) height to make F_1 plants that are *taller than either of the parents*. These F_1 plants were then selfed. What is the percentage of progeny in the F_2 generation that are shorter than the F_1 plants?

3. You cross homozygous pea plants with Tall (TT) and short (tt) height to make F_1 plants that are *taller than either of the parents*. These F_1 plants were then selfed. What is the percentage of progeny in the F_2 generation that are the same height as the short parent?

4. A couple is concerned that a rare autosomal recessive disease occurs in both of their families. Tests confirm that they are both carriers for a SNP that causes this disease, in which the wild-type 'A' is mutated to a 'G'. What is the chance any child will be a carrier?

5. A couple is concerned that a rare autosomal recessive disease occurs in both of their families. Tests confirm that they are both carriers for a SNP that causes this disease, in which the wild-type 'A' is mutated to a 'G'. What is the chance any child will be affected?

6. A couple is concerned that a rare autosomal recessive disease occurs in both of their families. Tests confirm that they are both carriers for a SNP that causes this disease, in which the wild-type 'A' is mutated to a 'G'. What is the chance any child will not be a carrier or affected?

7. A couple is concerned that a rare x-linked recessive disease occurs in the mothers family. Tests confirm that the mother is a carrier for a SNP that causes this disease. If they have a female child, what is the chance she will be a carrier?

8. A couple is concerned that a rare x-linked recessive disease occurs in the mothers family. Tests confirm that the mother is a carrier for a SNP that causes this disease. If they have a male child, what is the chance they will be a carrier?

9. In a cross between parent 1 AaBbCc x Parent 2 AaBbCc, what is the chance in fractions of a progeny having the genotype AABbCC?

10. Two unhealthy parents with similar symptoms have two unhealthy children with similar symptoms and one child that exhibits far more severe symptoms. What is the most likely cause?

Pedigree Worksheet 1 Student: _____ Section/Course:_____
Autosomal Recessive

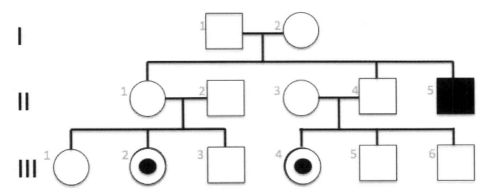

1. Indicate everyone who must be a carrier in the above RARE autosomal recessive pedigree

2. Assume II-5 finds a carrier mate. What percentage of their children will be carriers?

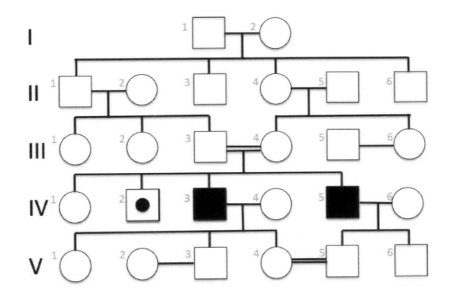

3. Who MUST be carriers in the above autosomal recessive pedigree

4. Who MIGHT be carriers in the above autosomal recessive pedigree

5. What century was generation I born in? (1800s, 1900s, 2000s) Why?

Pedigree Worksheet 2 Student: _____ Section/Course: _____
Autosomal Recessive

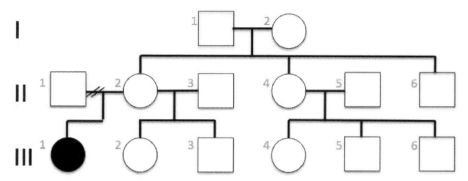

1   Who is the proband in the above autosomal recessive pedigree?

2   What is the relationship between II-1, II-2 and II-3 in the above autosomal recessive pedigree?

3   Who MUST be a carrier in the above autosomal recessive pedigree?

4   Who MIGHT be a carrier in the above autosomal recessive pedigree?

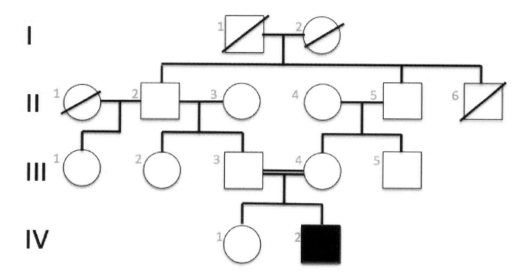

5   Who would you test in the above pedigree to see if they are carriers?

6   How could you determine whether I-1 or I-2 had been the carrier?

Pedigree Worksheet 3
Autosomal Dominant

Student: _____ Section/Course: _____

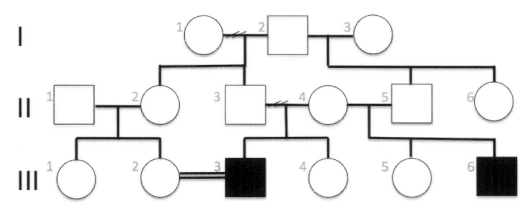

1   Who might have been affected in the above autosomal dominant pedigree?

2   What is the percent chance that a child from III-2 and III-3 will be affected?

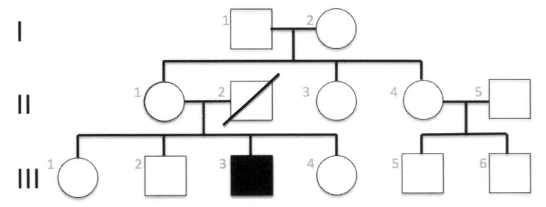

3   Who might have been affected in the above autosomal dominant pedigree?

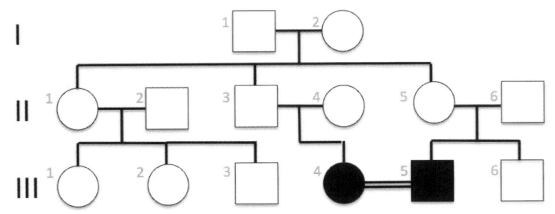

4   Who might have been affected in the above autosomal dominant pedigree?

5   What is the percent chance that a child from III-4 and III-5 will be affected?

Pedigree Worksheet 4
X-Linked Recessive

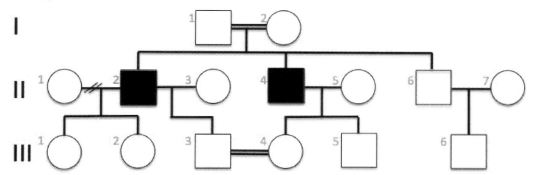

1. Who MUST be carriers in the above X-linked recessive pedigree?

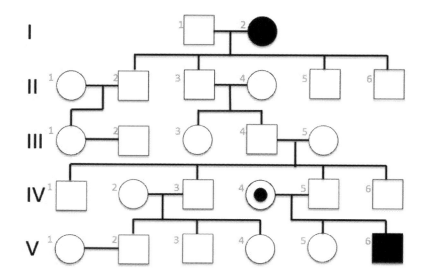

2. Who MUST be carriers in the above X-linked recessive pedigree?

3. Who MIGHT be carriers in this X-linked recessive pedigree?

4. Who MUST be affected in the above X-linked recessive pedigree?

Pedigree Worksheet 5
X-Linked Dominant

1. Who else MUST be/have been affected in the following X-linked dominant pedigree?

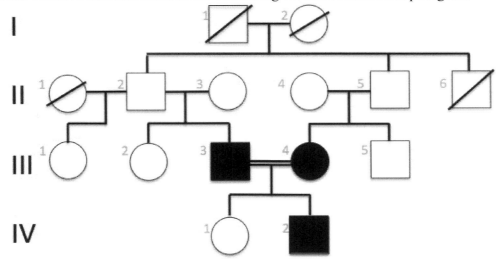

2. Who else MUST be/have been affected in the following X-linked dominant pedigree?

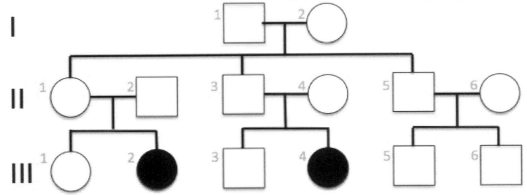

3. Who else MUST be/have been affected in the following X-linked dominant pedigree?

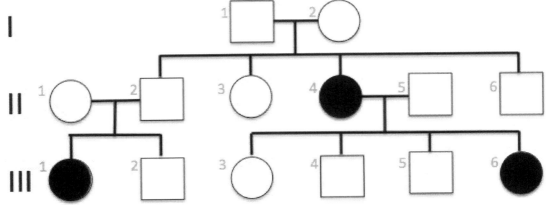

Pedigree Worksheet 6
SSR and SNP Pedigrees

Student: _____ Section/Course: _____

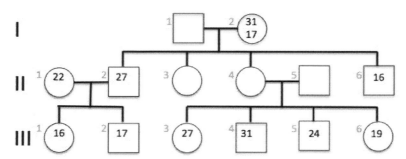

1. Complete as many genotypes as you can from the above pedigree (Homozygous SSRs indicated by 2 identical size entries)

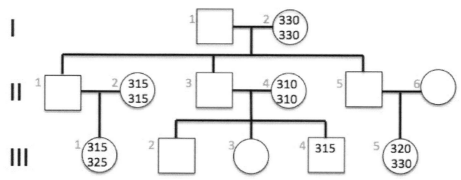

2. Complete as many genotypes as you can from the above pedigree (Homozygous SSRs indicated by 2 identical size entries):

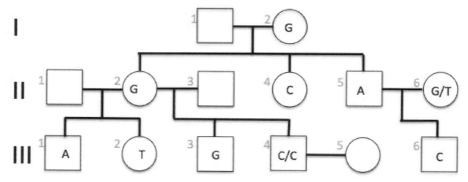

3. Identify all possible SNPs in the above Pedigree. I-1 and II-3 are homozygous. (Homozygous SNPs indicated by 2 identical nucleotide entries):

Pedigree Worksheet 7 Student: _____ Section/Course: _____
General Pedigrees

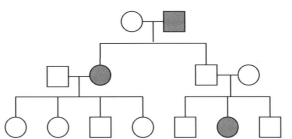

1   The pedigree above represents possible autosomal recessive inheritance (carriers not shown) (T/F)?   If False, why?

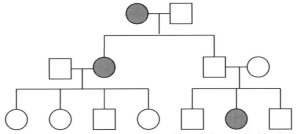

2   The pedigree above represents possible autosomal dominant inheritance (T/F)?   If False, why?

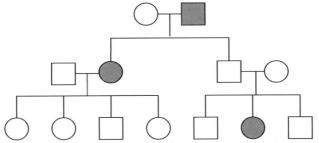

3   The pedigree above represents possible x-linked recessive inheritance (carriers not shown) (T/F)? If False, why?

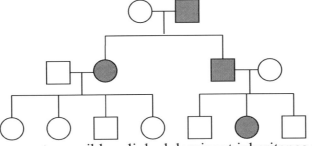

4   The pedigree above represents possible x-linked dominant inheritance (T/F)?   If False, why?

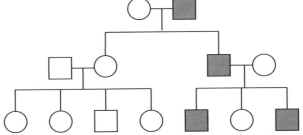

5   The pedigree above represents possible y-linked inheritance (T/F)?   If False, why?

How to Complete Forensics Worksheets

The Combined DNA Index System is a database that combines molecular data generated by multiple law enforcement agencies In order to consistently identify individuals who have committed crimes. The system utilizes 20 short tandem repeats (aka SSR and microsatellites, see below) and AMEL, a sex chromosome specific primer that produces a 212 bp combined allele fragment for females and 212 and 218 bp heterozygous fragments for males. *The function of CODIS data is to accurately separate individuals on a molecular basis.*

A molecular marker allows you to predict what form or function a specific DNA sequence has in a single individual. Molecular markers come in many forms, two of which are illustrated below (SNPs and SSRs). In humans, the most numerous of these markers are single nucleotide polymorphisms (SNPs). SNPs are used to determine whether an A, T, G or C is present at a particular bp location in the genome. Short Tandem Repeats (STRs), Simple Sequence Repeats (SSRs) or microsatellites are repeated DNA fragments of 1-6 bp that vary in copy number and thus *change the length* of that region of DNA. These size-based markers are what is used for CODIS fingerprinting and for paternity testing. Molecular markers are inherited just like any other trait in humans, thus they follow a Mendelian pattern of inheritance.

5'-ATCGAGTCAGTAG **C** AGTAGAGCTAGTACACAGTAGTA-3'	Wild Type
5'-ATCGAGTCAGTAG **T** AGTAGAGCTAGTACACAGTAGTA-3'	SNP; c.14C>T
5'-AGATAGACGAT **CAGCAGCAGCAG** GATACGTATCAG-3'	wild type CAG_4 SSR
5'-AGATAGACGAT **CAGCAGCAGCAGCAGCAG** GATACGTATCAG-3'	CAG_6 SSR

The form of the two most common molecular markers, Single nucleotide polymorphism (SNP) shown below the wild type (normal) sequence or as a variation in the wild type number of simple sequence repeats (SSR).

Every human receives their DNA from their parents - there is no random creation of genetic material - It is the combination of the alleles that we receive that makes us unique. Lets explore how this works; with only four different STR (SSR) loci, the graphic below shows how many combinations are possible in the same family.

Marker 1 (M1)

	22	24
22	22/22	22/24
24	22/24	24/24

Marker 2 (M2)

	17	17
17	17/17	17/17
18	17/18	17/18

Marker 3 (M3)

	13	15
12	12/13	12/15
14	13/14	14/15

Marker 4 (M4)

	8	10
9	8/9	9/10
10	8/10	10/10

We will say that your fingerprint is M1 22/24; M2 17/17; M3 14/15; and M4 9/10; What is the chance that a brother or sister will have the same alleles for these four markers? The math is simple - there are four possibilities for the two parents for each marker, so it is either 1/4, 1/2, or 1/1 (all children have the same allele for this marker) and these possible combinations are multiplied by each other. The shaded Punnett squares below represent your fingerprint; *The fractions represent the likelihood of a sibling inheriting the same allele combination from your shared parents.*

Marker 1 (M1)			Marker 2 (M2)			Marker 3 (M3)			Marker 4 (M4)		
	22	24		17	17		13	15		8	10
22	22/22	22/24	17	17/17	17/17	12	12/13	12/15	9	8/9	9/10
24	22/24	24/24	18	17/18	17/18	14	13/14	14/15	10	8/10	10/10

$$\frac{1}{2} \times \frac{1}{2} \times \frac{1}{4} \times \frac{1}{4} = \frac{1}{64}$$

M1 — 22/24 are 1/2 of the possible combinations from these two parents

M2 — 17/17 are 1/2 of the possible combinations from these two parents

M3 — 14/15 are 1/4 of the possible combinations from these two parents

M4 — 9/10 are 1/4 of the possible combinations from these two parents

> *On average*, your parents would need to have about *64 children* before they would have another with an identical combination to yours for *only* these 4 markers - there are *20* CODIS markers and separating male and female siblings using the Amel sex-identification marker would increase this to *1/128* (1/64 x 1/2 = 1/128).

OK, so DNA fingerprinting can separate brothers and sisters - There are over seven *Billion* people on this planet, why do you hear all about the "One in a billion" chance of a match? In a familial test, you are only dealing with four possible alleles for each marker - two for each parent. *Period*. The truly useful feature of STR/SSR molecular markers is the fact that each one can have several different sizes within the worlds' population, with most of the CODIS markers having more than 10 possible sizes. This means that the Punnett square is 10x10, not 2x2 as shown above. Even better, each allele is represented at a different percentage in the population based on ethnicity, so that calculating random probability requires software…..but that isn't going to stop us!

Using 4 markers again, lets see how you do in a population as opposed to just your family. The frequencies below are for a both Caucasian and African American individuals and represent the actual CODIS marker set.

STR	Alleles	Frequency Caucasian*	Frequency African American*	Combination (Ca / AA)
D16S539	8/11	2(0.0198)(0.2723)	2(0.0361)(0.2933)	0.0107/0.0211
D21S11	27/31	2(0.0446)(0.0718)	2(0.0574)(0.0909)	0.0064/0.0104
D7S820	7/9	2(0.0173)(0.1460)	2(0.0072)(0.1579)	0.0050/0.0022
D3S1358	14/14	(0.1386)(0.1386)	(0.1220)(0.1220)	0.0192/0.0148

*Moretti, Tamyra R. et al. 2016. Population data on the expanded CODIS core STR loci for eleven populations of significance for forensic DNA analyses in the United States. Forensic Science International: Genetics, Volume 25, 175 - 181
You can find a full report of population-specific alleles in appendix A of the paper at:
https://www.fsigenetics.com/article/S1872-4973(16)30142-9/fulltext

You then multiply all of the combination frequencies to get 6.57408×10^{-009} or about 1 in 160 million Caucasians; The number within the African American population is about 1 in 140 million, or only slightly less rare…

Forensics 1 Student: _____ Section/Course: _____

1 ___ A CODIS fingerprint value of "15" means:
    A   There is a "15" chance of a match   D   There are 15 alleles
    B   There are 15 repeats in BOTH alleles   E   None of the above
    C   There are 15 individuals who match

2 ___ A CODIS fingerprint value of "15/18" means:
    A   There is a "15" chance of a match   D   There are 15 alleles
    B   There are 15 repeats in BOTH alleles   E   None of the above
    C   There are 15 and 18 individuals who match

3 ___ A CODIS fingerprint value of "245/259" means:
    A   There is a "245" chance of a match
    B   There are alleles with 245 and 259 repeats respectively
    C   There are 245 and 259 base pairs in the two alleles
    D   There are 245 alleles
    E   None of the above

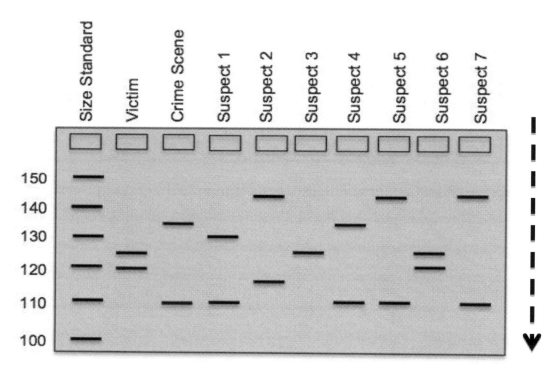

4 ___ Use the above autosomal single SSR marker data generated between several suspects, a victim and the crime scene to answer the following question. The arrow indicates direction of electrophoresis. Assuming HOMOZYGOUS PARENTS - Which of the following suspects could be brothers or sisters to the victim? BE VERY CAREFUL!
    A   Suspect 3 and Suspect 6
    B   Suspect 6
    C   Suspect 7 and Suspect 5
    D   All could be brothers or sisters
    E   None can be related

Forensics 2 Student: _____ Section/Course: _____

1 ___ A CODIS fingerprint value of "15/15" means:
    A   There are 15 individuals who match   D   There are 15 alleles
    B   The individuals are 15 years old   E   None of the above
    C   The parents of the suspect are homozygous for the 15 allele

2 ___ Identical twins will have the same CODIS fingerprint:
    A   Only if their parents are homozygous   D   Only at birth
    B   All of their lives   E   None of the above
    C   Unless one of them undergoes gender re-assignment

3 ___ A CODIS fingerprint match usually proves:
    A   The suspect is guilty
    B   The victim is related to the suspect
    C   The suspect's DNA was at the crime scene
    D   The suspect was involved in planning the crime
    E   None of the above

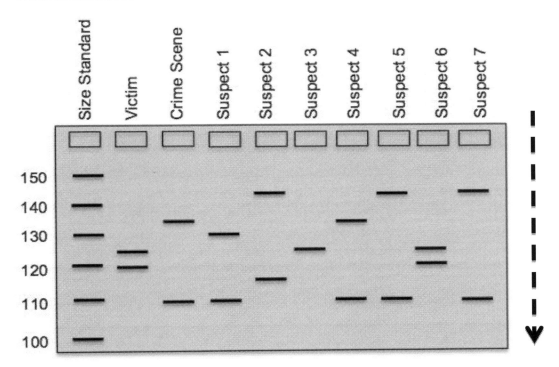

4 ___ Use the above autosomal single SSR marker data generated between several suspects, a victim and the crime scene to answer the following question. The arrow indicates direction of electrophoresis. Which of the following suspects could be brothers or sisters to the victim? BE VERY CAREFUL!
    A   Suspect 3 and Suspect 6
    B   Suspect 6
    C   Suspect 7 and Suspect 5
    D   All could be brothers or sisters
    E   None can be related

Forensics 3 Student: _____ Section/Course: _____

1. Draw the following single molecular marker fingerprints onto the agarose gel below:

Victim 120/140   Crime Scene 110/130
Suspect 1 130/130 Suspect 2 130/145   Suspect 3 110/145   Suspect 4 120/145
Suspect 5 130/145 Suspect 6 115/140   Suspect 7 130/130

2. Based on the data above, which band size is most likely the wild type (most common in the population)?

   130

3. Based on the data above, which band size is most likely the rarest in the population)?

   115

4. Using these data as a population, what percent of the alleles is your answer for #2?

   7/20 = **35%**

5. Using these data as a population, what percent of the alleles is your answer for #3?

   1/20 = **5%**

6. Who is the most likely suspect based on the fingerprints?

   Suspect 3 (only suspect carrying the rare 110 allele found at the crime scene)

Forensics 4   Student: _____   Section/Course: _____

Victim 140/140   Crime Scene 140/150
Suspect 1 130/130   Suspect 2 130/145   Suspect 3 110/145   Suspect 4 120/120
Suspect 5 130/145   Suspect 6 115/140   Suspect 7 120/130

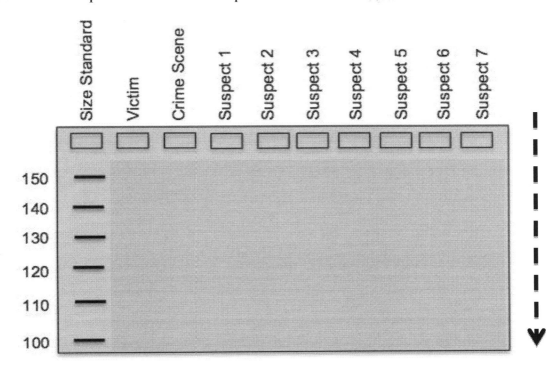

2 Based on the data above, which band size is most likely the wild type (most common in the population)?

3 Based on the data above, which band size is most likely the rarest in the population)?

4 Using these data as a population, what percent of the alleles is your answer for #2?

5 Using these data as a population, what percent of the alleles is your answer for #3?

6 Who is the most likely suspect based on the fingerprints?

How to Complete Paternity Worksheets

Paternity is extremely similar to forensics – with the simple exception that instead of correlating a potential world of samples, paternity testing is focused on eliminating the possibility of relationship between a father and a child. A simple mis-match is all that is necessary. The Combined DNA Index System molecular markers are used to screen each subject. The system utilizes 20 short tandem repeats (aka SSR and microsatellites, see below). *The function of CODIS data is to accurately separate individuals on a molecular basis.*

A molecular marker allows you to predict what form or function a specific DNA sequence has in a single individual. Short Tandem Repeats (STRs), Simple Sequence Repeats (SSRs) or microsatellites are repeated DNA fragments of 1-6 bp that vary in copy number and thus *change the length* of that region of DNA. These size-based markers are used for paternity testing. Molecular markers are inherited just like any other trait in human; thus they follow a Mendelian pattern of inheritance.

5'-ATCGAGTCAGTAG C AGTAGAGCTAGTACACAGTAGTA-3'	Wild Type
5'-ATCGAGTCAGTAG T AGTAGAGCTAGTACACAGTAGTA-3'	SNP; c.14C>T
5'-AGATAGACGAT CAGCAGCAGCAG GATACGTATCAG-3'	wild type CAG_4 SSR
5'-AGATAGACGAT CAGCAGCAGCAGCAGCAG GATACGTATCAG-3'	CAG_6 SSR

The form of the two most common molecular markers, Single nucleotide polymorphism (SNP) shown below the wild type (normal) sequence or as a variation in the wild type number of simple sequence repeats (SSR).

Every human receives their DNA from their parents - there is no random creation of genetic material - It is the combination of the alleles that we receive that makes us unique. Lets explore how this works; with only four different STR (SSR) loci, the graphic below shows how many combinations are possible in the same family.

In a familial test, you are only dealing with four possible alleles for each marker - two for each parent. *Period.* When you investigate paternity, you are truly checking on thing – can the alleles of a child come from the tested parent? Since child 3 has the 220/237 alleles for TPOX, only Father 1 could have provided one of these alleles (220). This *does not* prove that father 1 is the parent of child 3, but it is sufficient evidence to *eliminate* potential fathers 2 and 3, since *neither* of them has allele 220 or 237.

Marker	Child 1	Child 2	Child 3	Product	Father 1	Father 2	Father 3
TPOX	216/220	227/237	220/237	216-264	220/220	216	227/260
D3S1358	99/147	99/112	147	99-147	130/147	130/147	112/134
FGA	158/300	246/300	300	158-314	158/300	158/314	246

Determining the Mothers Alleles
Circle the alleles from the determined father 1 in all children. You are simply selecting alleles that *had* to come from the father - in other words, for TPOX in child 1 the alleles are 216 and 220, but their father only has 220 and 220 - thus the 220 allele *must* come from father 1. Circle all alleles from each father in this manner - what is left is what *must* have come from the mother. In the case of FGA, CSF1PO, D7S820 and TH01, it is unclear as to whether the mother is homozygous for the allele indicated or if her second allele was simply not transmitted to any of her three children.

Paternity 1   Student: _____ Section/Course: _____

Marker	Child 1	Child 2	Child 3	Product	Father 1	Father 2	Father 3
TPOX	216/220	227/237	220/237	216-264	220/220	216	227/260
D3S1358	99/147	99/112	147	99-147	130/147	130/147	112/134
FGA	158/300	246/300	300	158-314	158/300	158/314	246
D5S818	129/165	136/154	129/136	129-177	129/177	129/177	130/154
CSF1PO	316/320	312/320	320	287-331	316/320	287/320	294/312
D7S820	194/216	234/234	194/200	194-234	200/216	200	234
D8S1179	157/209	160/182	185/209	157-209	157/185	157/185	182/203
TH01	171/184	184	171/184	171-215	171	171/215	184/206
VWA	160	136/160	122/130	122-182	130/160	130	136/163
D16S539	156/280	129/177	129/349	129-177	280/349	129/349	163/177
D18S51	284/322	309/320	284/322	262-349	322	262/300	309
D21S11	164/272	194/242	180/242	154-272	180/272	180	194/235

Allele sizes reported in ascending order and do not indicate parental source. Product is the size range for the marker. *Assume that the mother is the same for all three children.*

1   Based on the paternity data above, who is the father for child 1?

2   Based on the paternity data above, who is the father for child 2?

3   Based on the paternity data above, who is the father for child 3?

4   Based on the identified fathers, what is the mothers genotype for TPOX?

5   Based on the identified fathers, what is the mothers genotype for D5S818?

6   Based on the identified fathers, what is the mothers genotype for VWA?

7   If you have three siblings from two parents, how could you prove shared paternity (In other words, could you be sure that all three had the same father) without testing the parents?

Paternity 2 Student: _____ Section/Course: _____

Marker	Child 1	Child 2	Child 3	Product	Father 1	Father 2	Father 3
TPOX	216/220	227/237	220/237	216-264	220/220	216	227/260
D3S1358	99/147	99/112	147	99-147	130/147	130/147	112/134
FGA	158/300	246/300	300	158-314	158/300	158/314	246
D5S818	129/165	136/154	129/136	129-177	129/177	129/177	130/154
CSF1PO	316/320	312/320	320	287-331	316/320	287/320	294/312
D7S820	194/216	234/234	194/200	194-234	200/216	200	234
D8S1179	157/209	160/182	185/209	157-209	157/185	157/185	182/203
TH01	171/184	184	171/184	171-215	171	171/215	184/206
VWA	160	136/160	122/130	122-182	130/160	130	136/163
D16S539	156/280	129/177	129/349	129-177	280/349	129/349	163/177
D18S51	284/322	309/320	284/322	262-349	322	262/300	309
D21S11	164/272	194/242	180/242	154-272	180/272	180	194/235

Allele sizes reported in ascending order and do not indicate parental source. Product is the size range for the marker. *Assume that the mother is the same for all three children.*

1   Based on the paternity data above, who is the father for child 1?

2   Based on the paternity data above, who is the father for child 2?

3   Based on the paternity data above, who is the father for child 3?

4   Based on the identified fathers, what is the mothers genotype for D18S51?

5   Based on the identified fathers, what is the mothers genotype for D3S1358?

6   Based on the identified fathers, what is the mothers genotype for FGA?

7   Although this type of test is designed to determine paternity, it can also be used to determine maternity. Can you think of two examples of when this may be required?

Paternity 3 Student: _____ Section/Course: _____

1   You suspect that your sister is adopted. Assuming you have a sample of her DNA, which combination of individuals' DNA could you test to determine if she *is* your sister?

        A   Your mother and your father. Yes ___ No ___
               Why/How?

        B   Your mother and your maternal grandparents. Yes ___ No ___
               Why/How?

        C   Your mother and your four maternal aunts. Yes ___ No ___
               Why/How?

        D   Your paternal grandparents. Yes ___ No ___
               Why/How?

        E   Your maternal grandparents. Yes ___ No ___
               Why/How?

        F   You and your three brothers. Yes ___ No ___
               Why/How?

        G   Your maternal and paternal grandparents. Yes ___ No ___
               Why/How?

Paternity 4   Student: _____   Section/Course: _____

1. Use the simple sequence repeat (SSR) genotypes below to complete the pedigree, then answer the remaining questions.

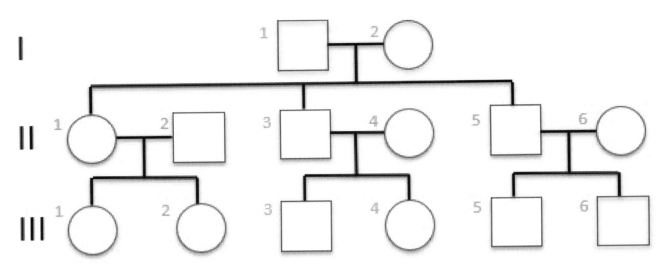

I-1 110/135, I-2 140/140, II-1 110/140, II-2 120/140, II-3 135/140, II-4 130/130, II-5 110/140, II-6 130/130, III-1 110/120, III-2 140/140, III-3 130/135, III-4 135/140, III-5 110/120, III-6 130/140

2. What are the remaining two allele combinations for parents II-1 and II-2?

3. What are the remaining possible allele combinations for parents I-1 and II-2?

4. There are two children in this pedigree who have different parents than indicated; Who are they and why are they not the offspring of the indicated parents?

5. How many different alleles are represented in this pedigree for SSR marker 1? List them…

6. How many of the alleles in question 5 *cannot* be passed on to the next generation of this family?

40

How to Complete Alleles in a Population Worksheets

Determining the composition or percentage of an allele in a population is relatively easy. Using the formula $p^2 + 2pq + q^2 = 1.0$ you can identify how many homozygous (pp or qq genotypes) or heterozygous (pq) individuals are in the population. For example, say that you know that 10% of the alleles in the population are the q allele, the following calculations give you the remaining information:

$p^2 + 2pq + q^2 = 1.0$

$p^2 + 2p(0.1) + (0.1)^2 = 1.0$ — *Add the value for "q" alleles into the formula*

$(0.9)^2 + 2(0.9)(0.1) + (0.1)^2 = 1.0$ — *Since p + q must equal 1.0, you can derive that p must equal 0.9*

0.81 (81%)   +   0.18 (18%)   +   0.01 (1%) = 1.0
Homozygous   heterozygous   homozygous
pp individuals   pq individuals   qq individuals

Now try the same with the q allele represented in 40% of the population

$(0.6)^2 + 2(0.6)(0.4) + (0.4)^2 = 1.0$ — *Since p + q must equal 1.0, you can derive that p must equal 0.6*

0.36 (36%)   +   0.48 (48%)   +   0.16 (16%) = 1.0
Homozygous   heterozygous   homozygous
pp individuals   pq individuals   qq individuals

Add the numbers that you have - if they add up to 1.0 you have probably done the calculations correctly.

Why do we care? Using this formula allows you to calculate the number of carriers and unaffected individuals in a population based on how many individuals *have the disease.*

Within the Amish community, the current incidence rate Ellis van-creveld disease (dwarfism an/or polydactyly) is one in 200. When compared to one in 60,000-200,000 in the general population, this is a very high rate. Calculate what the percent of carriers in the Amish population is using the known homozygous individuals (0.5%; 1 in 200).

Working backwards, you know that 1 in 200 is 0.5% or 0.005; the square root of 0.005 is 0.07; complete the calculations to find the percent of carriers and homozygous unaffected individuals in the population....

    ? %   ? %   0.5%
homozygous   heterozygous   homozygous
unaffected   EVC carriers   EVC individuals

$p^2 + 2pq + .005 = 1.0$ ($q^2 = 0.005$; **q = 0.07**) — *add the value for "q" alleles into the formula*

$(0.93)^2 + 2(0.93)(0.07) + 0.005 = 1.0$ — *Use the fact that p + q must equal 1.0*

   86.5%   **13%**   **0.5%**
homozygous   heterozygous   homozygous
unaffected   **EVC carriers**   **EVC affected**

Alleles in a Population 1   Student: _____   Section/Course:_____

1. ___ Disease A is autosomal recessive. A total of 16% of the study population of 100 people are affected. How many carriers are in the study population?
   - A 12
   - B 24
   - C 36
   - D 48
   - E 60

2. ___ Disease A is autosomal recessive. A total of 36% of the study population of 100 people are affected. How many homozygous unaffected individuals are in the study population?
   - A 16
   - B 32
   - C 48
   - D 64
   - E 80

3. ___ A population of 1000 people has 40 individuals who are affected by an autosomal recessive disease. How many are homozygous unaffected?
   - A 32
   - B 256
   - C 320
   - D 640
   - E 810

4. ___ A population of 1000 people has 40 individuals who are affected by an autosomal recessive disease. How many are heterozygous unaffected?
   - A 32
   - B 256
   - C 320
   - D 640
   - E 810

5. ___ A population of 100 people has 4 individuals who are affected by an autosomal recessive disease. How many are homozygous unaffected?
   - A 32
   - B 26
   - C 48
   - D 64
   - E 81

6. ___ A population of 20 people has 5 individuals who are affected by an autosomal recessive disease. How many are homozygous unaffected?
   - A 5
   - B 10
   - C 15
   - D 20
   - E Unable to determine

7. ___ A population of 20 people has 5 individuals who are affected by an autosomal recessive disease. How many are heterozygous unaffected?
   - A 5
   - B 10
   - C 15
   - D 20
   - E Unable to determine

Alleles in a Population 2   Student: _____   Section/Course: _____

1. Disease A is autosomal recessive. A total of 16% of the study population of 100 people are affected. How many heterozygous unaffected people are in the study population?

2. Disease A is autosomal dominant. A total of 36% of the study population of 100 people are affected. How many homozygous unaffected people are in the study population?

3. Disease A is autosomal dominant. A total of 36% of the study population of 100 people are affected. How many heterozygous affected people are in the study population?

4. Disease A is autosomal recessive. A total of 91% of the study population of 100 people are unaffected. How many heterozygous carrier people are in the study population?

5. Disease A is autosomal recessive. A total of 1% of the study population of 100 people are affected. How many homozygous affected people are in the study population?

6. Disease A is autosomal recessive. A total of 1% of the study population of 100 people are affected. How many heterozygous unaffected people are in the study population?

Calculator Required

7. Disease A is autosomal recessive. A total of 0.005% of the study population of 100 people are affected (1 in 200 people). How many homozygous unaffected people are in the study population?

8. Cystic Fibrosis is autosomal recessive. About 1 in 3,000 Caucasians are affected (http://ghr.nlm.nih.gov/condition/cystic-fibrosis; 1/2019). What percent of the study population are homozygous unaffected?

9. Cystic Fibrosis is autosomal recessive. About 1 in 3,000 Caucasians are affected (http://ghr.nlm.nih.gov/condition/cystic-fibrosis; 1/2019). What percent of the study population are unaffected?

Alleles in a Population 3   Student: _____   Section/Course:_____

1. Disease A is autosomal recessive. A total of 16% of the study population of 100 people are affected. How many homozygous unaffected people are in the study population?

2. Disease A is autosomal recessive. A total of 16% of the study population of 100 people are affected. How many unaffected people are in the study population?

3. Disease A is autosomal dominant. A total of 36% of the study population of 100 people are affected. How many homozygous affected people are in the study population?

4. Disease A is autosomal recessive. A total of 91% of the study population of 100 people are unaffected. How many affected people are in the study population?

5. Disease A is autosomal recessive. A total of 91% of the study population of 100 people are unaffected. How many homozygous unaffected people are in the study population?

6. Disease A is autosomal recessive. A total of 1% of the study population of 100 people are affected. How many homozygous unaffected people are in the study population?

Calculator Required

7. Disease A is autosomal recessive. A total of 0.005% of the study population of 100 people are affected (1 in 200 people). How many heterozygous unaffected people are in the study population?

8. Disease A is autosomal recessive. A total of 0.005% of the study population of 100 people are affected (1 in 200 people). How many unaffected people are in the study population?

9. Cystic Fibrosis is autosomal recessive. About 1 in 3,000 Caucasians are affected (http://ghr.nlm.nih.gov/condition/cystic-fibrosis; 1/2019). What percent of the study population are heterozygous carriers?

How to Use Pull and Present Worksheets in a Class

The "Pull and Present" in-class exercise forces students to quickly identify publications that satisfy a random assignment from the instructor. I typically use two terms, a technique and an organism, but this of course can be modified as the instructor sees fit.

I cut out the following list into strips, which are then placed in two cups. I typically select the first two slips, then do the first presentation before passing out the slips to students, as this demonstration allows the students to see what is expected of them.

After the instructor demonstration, each student picks a slip from each cup. They are then given 5 minutes to find a publication abstract (PubMed or PubMed Central are good websites for this), that includes *both* items. They must now complete the pull and present worksheet. When the five minutes have expired, each of them must turn off their computers/stop working on their worksheets. Now, the instructor pulls a student name from a third cup. The selected student must then present their information to the class, identifying what they answered for each question and *why*. This is typically a multiple day exercise – until all students have completed the exercise – with a new organism/technique required every day from all students. I have used this for smaller enrollment courses – typically Advanced, Honors or Graduate Genetics with up to 14 students enrolled.

In addition, peer-based grading can be an aspect of this exercise, as this emphasizes the peer-based review nature of science. I have used a minimum of one 8 and one 9 out of ten to reduce students only giving 10's to their peers. I have also placed a "7" minimum to reduce the possibility of a student getting all 0's - - just remember that this is a *learning* exercise, *not* a punitive one.

Homo sapiens	SSR
Drosophila melanogaster	Microsatellites
Danio rerio	SNP
Arabidopsis thaliana	SNP
Saccharomyces cerevisiae	SNP
Penguin	RFLP
Elephant	RNAi
Caenorhabditis elegans	Knockout
Mus Musculus	Knockdown
Pan troglodytes	Fingerprinting
Ustilago maydis	Sequencing
Lotus japonicus	Sequencing
Medicago truncatula	Sequencing
Oryza sativa	Transcript
Cat	mRNA
Chicken	Mutation
Dog	Mutation
Rat	Population
Rhesus macaque	Migration
Naked mole rat	Pedigree

Pull and Present 1   Student: _____   Section/Course:_____

Organism   _____   Trait/technique   _____

Number of Articles   _____

PubMed/PubMed Central or OMIM ID Number   _____

Authors   _____ et al

Why was research performed? _____

Which sub-disciplines of genetics are indicated in the abstract?

	Line	Keywords
Central Dogma	_____	_____
Transmission	_____	_____
HW/Population	_____	_____

Most important Hardy-Weinberg assumption violated?   _____

Using Hardy-Weinberg, propose a new research project that could continue the presented work

_____

_____

Presenters (You must give at least one 8 and one 9)

Name _____   Name _____

Score (7-10) _____   Score (7-10) _____

-------------------------------------   -------------------------------------

Name _____   Name _____

Score (7-10) _____   Score (7-10) _____

-------------------------------------   -------------------------------------

Name _____   Name _____

Score (7-10) _____   Score (7-10) _____

-------------------------------------   -------------------------------------

Pull and Present 2   Student: _____   Section/Course: _____

Organism _____   Trait/technique _____

Number of Articles _____

PubMed/PubMed Central or OMIM ID Number _____

Authors _____ et al

Why was research performed? _____

Number of subjects studied? _____

What type of data was collected? _____

What type of null control did they use? _____

What is the weakest aspect of this study? _____ line of Abstract _____

Using Hardy-Weinberg, propose a new research project that could continue the presented work

_____

_____

Presenters (You must give at least one 8 and one 9)

Name _____   Name _____

Score (7-10) _____   Score (7-10) _____

------------------------------------- -------------------------------------

Name _____   Name _____

Score (7-10) _____   Score (7-10) _____

------------------------------------- -------------------------------------

Name _____   Name _____

Score (7-10) _____   Score (7-10) _____

------------------------------------- -------------------------------------

Crossword Puzzle 1

Across

4 Occurs in CG-rich DNA sequences
5 Generate ATP for cell function
7 Very common mating cause of rare autosomal recessive disease
8 Field of Biology concerned with the structure function and evolution of genomes
11 A, T, G or C
13 Gene copies from a common ancestor
14 A group of genes affecting a single trait
15 A founder of population genetics

Down

1 A measured trait that can be influenced by the environment
2 The separation of DNA strands using heat
3 This must be random in a population at equilibrium
6 The addition of a base pair in a sequence
9 Small circular genome in plants
10 Draw liquid into a pipettor
12 Change over time

Created at crosswordhobbyist.com by JL Shultz

Crossword Puzzle 2 Student: _____ Section/Course: _____

Across

1 Gene copies from within the same genome
3 Database of biomedical papers
5 A mutant that has changed back to the wild type
7 The genetic makeup of Human gametes
9 Multiple alleles interact to create a trait
10 Trisomy 18
13 Exhibit "luck of the draw" inheritance in humans
14 Loss of genetic variability in a small population

Down

2 Cells that are passed on to next generation
3 One gene creates multiple effects
4 Another term for researcher
6 The end of a chromosome
8 The loss of a base pair in a sequence
11 This codon means that a frame is not open
12 Compare Protein sequences

Created at crosswordhobbyist.com by JL Shultz

49

Crossword Puzzle 3

Student: _____ Section/Course: _____

Across

3 A formed cavity in an agarose gel for sample loading
4 Non-disjunction during development
9 Phenotype not caused by mutation(s)
11 A marker based on repeat sequences
12 A purine is switched to a pyrimidine or vice-versa
13 Marking one parents DNA via methylation for selective expression
14 Spreading your sample across growth media

Down

1 Evolution in which a species changes over time
2 The amount of phenotype caused by mutation
5 A molecular marker based around a repeat sequence
6 An organism that uses genes from closely related species
7 Mapping that combines multiple traits and molecular markers
8 Mendelian genetics aka
10 The removal of one or two bases in an exon

Created at crosswordhobbyist.com by JL Shultz

Crossword Puzzle 4

Across

1. A single piece of DNA containing genes
3. A fragment of foreign DNA stored in a yeast-based genome
4. A change in DNA sequence
6. Multiple alleles interact to create a trait
7. These elements may interrupt a gene and cause lack of function
8. A difference between two samples
11. Critically evaluate research
12. The top of a fragment in capillary detection
13. A region of DNA that has relatively more mutations than other regions

Down

2. Evolution in which a new species is formed
4. Having one chromosome due to non-disjunction
5. Cells with a nucleus
9. DNA sequence in front of gene
10. The most common Human molecular marker

Created at crosswordhobbyist.com by JL Shultz

Lab-Based Exercise 1
Safety and Pipetting

Student: _____ Section/Course: _____

1. The fire extinguisher is located:

2. The number to call in an emergency:

3. The first aid box is located:

4. The eyewash is located:

5. I should avoid skin contact with ethidium bromide (T/F)

6. Which of the following is a common danger in a molecular genetics laboratory?
   - A Ethidium Bromide
   - B Poison
   - C Solar radiation
   - D Open flame
   - E None of the above

7. Which of the following is a common danger in a molecular genetics laboratory?
   - A Solar radiation
   - B Poison
   - C High Voltage
   - D Open flame
   - E None of the above

8. What are the four basic functions of a pipettor (4 pts)?

9. You have pipetted an unknown volume of water onto the scale, which reads

    0.8738 g   How much have you transferred? _____ ul

10. You have pipetted an unknown volume of water onto the scale, which reads

    0.0034 g   How much have you transferred? _____ ul

11. Which of the following weighs more?
    - A 2.1 ml water
    - B 0.002 L water
    - C 2.1 mg
    - D 2,150 ul water
    - E 5.002 nm

Lab-Based Exercise 2 Student: _____ Section/Course: _____
Basic PCR/DNA

1. The fire extinguisher is located:

2. The number to call in an emergency:

3. The first aid box is located:

4. DNA runs to the negative (black) end of an electrophoresis gel (T/F)

5. PCR stops when the template DNA is used up (T/F)

6. DNA separation in PCR happens at 100° F (T/F)

7. Genomic DNA includes introns (T/F)

8. PCR doubles the amount of target DNA with each cycle (T/F)

9. Detection of basic PCR is typically accomplished via some form of electrophoresis (T/F)

10. In PCR, as cycle number increases, product quantity increases (T/F)

11. DNA has a positive charge (T/F)

12. Name 5 components of a PCR reaction (5pts)

13. You have just run a PCR reaction in a thermal cycler. You attempt to load into an agarose gel but find that your PCR tubes are empty. What could be the cause?
    - A The components of the reaction ran out
    - B The heated lid was not on
    - C You forgot to put DNA into the reaction
    - D You used the wrong pipettor
    - E All of the above

14. What would happen to the samples in the following PCR reaction?
    Lid 93°; Wait; Auto
    95° 5 min
    95° 30 sec
    40° 60 sec
    72° 30 sec
    Goto 2 Rep 40 times
    72° 5 minutes
    Hold 4°

Lab-Based Exercise 3 Student: _____ Section/Course: _____
Hybridization

1. The fire extinguisher is located:

2. The number to call in an emergency:

3. The eyewash is located:

4. You wish to design primers with a high T_m. Which of the following sequences has the highest T_m?
   - A 5' - CGCCTTATTG - 3'
   - B 5' - ATCATAGGCG - 3'
   - C 3' - TAGTATAACC - 5'
   - D 5' - TAGTACAACC - 3'
   - E 3' - TCTTCCGCGT - 5'

5. The *Hind*III enzyme recognizes the following sequence 5'-AAGCTT -3'. Approximately how many times will it cut a random DNA sequence of 100,000 bp?
   - A 4
   - B 6
   - C 12
   - D 25
   - E None of the above

6. The *Hae*III enzyme recognizes the following sequence 5'-GGCC -3'. Approximately how many times will it cut a random DNA sequence of 1,000 bp?
   - A 4
   - B 6
   - C 12
   - D 25
   - E None of the above

7. You have designed a 10 bp PCR primer. How many random base pairs are needed to match this sequence?
   - A 10 bp
   - B 1,000 bp
   - C 1,000,000 bp
   - D 1,000,000,000 bp
   - E 1,000,000,000,000 bp

8. You have designed a 15 bp PCR primer. How many random base pairs are needed to match this sequence?
   - A 10 bp
   - B 1,000 bp
   - C 1,000,000 bp
   - D 1,000,000,000 bp
   - E 1,000,000,000,000 bp

9. You have designed a 20 bp PCR primer. How many random base pairs are needed to match this sequence?
   - A 10 bp
   - B 1,000 bp
   - C 1,000,000 bp
   - D 1,000,000,000 bp
   - E 1,000,000,000,000 bp

Lab-Based Exercise 4
DNA Analysis

Student: _____ Section/Course: _____

1. You wish to design primers with a low T_m. Which of the following sequences has the lowest T_m?
   - A   5' - CGCCTTATTG - 3'
   - B   5' - ATCATAGGCG - 3'
   - C   3' - TAGTATAACC - 5'
   - D   5' - TAGTACAACC - 3'
   - E   3' - TCTTCCGCGT - 5'

2. The genomic sequence of a gene is 10,000 bp long, the edited mRNA is 3,000 bp long and the polypeptide is 930 amino acids long. How many codons are in the edited mRNA?
   - A   2,790
   - B   930
   - C   310
   - D   6
   - E   Unable to determine

3. The genomic sequence of a gene is 10,000 bp long, the edited mRNA is 3,000 bp long and the polypeptide is 930 amino acids long. How many base pairs are in codons?
   - A   2,790
   - B   930
   - C   310
   - D   6
   - E   Unable to determine

4. The genomic sequence of a gene is 10,000 bp long, the edited mRNA is 3,000 bp long and the polypeptide is 310 amino acids long. How many codons are in the edited mRNA?
   - A   2,790
   - B   930
   - C   310
   - D   6
   - E   Unable to determine

5. You wish to identify an unknown bacterial sample. Which database would be the most effective to search?
   - A   Standard non-redundant
   - B   rna/ITS
   - C   Human Genomic + transcript
   - D   Model
   - E   Unable to determine

6. This procedure results in fragments of DNA with specific ends
   - A   PCR
   - B   Colony PCR
   - C   Electrophoresis
   - D   Pipetting
   - E   Bioinformatics

7. This procedure results in fragments of DNA with specific ends
   - A   DNA extraction
   - B   Restriction digest
   - C   Electrophoresis
   - D   Pipetting
   - E   Bioinformatics

8. This procedure results in fragments of DNA without specific ends
   - A   PCR
   - B   Restriction digest
   - C   Electrophoresis
   - D   Pipetting
   - E   DNA extraction

Super-Matching 1 Student: _____ Section/Course: _____
Laboratory

Agar	Free from bacteria or other living organisms
Agarose	Cavity in an agarose gel for sample loading
Annealing	Creates agarose wells for sample loading
Band	Used to transfer small amounts of liquid
Blot	Grow bacteria under specific conditions
Centrifuge	Copy DNA using temperature cycling
Chamber	Fragment of DNA used to start PCR
Colony	Allows detection of DNA in a gel
Comb	Combined sample after spinning
Denaturation	A dish best served to bacteria
Dispense	Expel liquid from a pipettor
Enzyme	DNA base pair matching
Evaporation	Cleave/cut a molecule
Hybridization	Electrophoresis matrix
Incubate	Catalyzes a reaction
Ladder	Reset a scale
PCR	Growth media
Peak	Remove excess liquid
Pellet	Primers attach to DNA in PCR
Petri	Separates samples by spinning
Pipette	Prevented by a heated lid in PCR
Primer	Size standard for electrophoresis
Restriction	Similar-sized fragments on a gel
Sanger	Multiple copies of a single bacteria
Sterile	Oldest still viable sequencing method
Streak	Separation of DNA strands using heat
Tare	Holds running buffer for electrophoresis
Transilluminator	Top of a fragment in capillary detection
Well	Spreading your sample across growth media

Super-Matching 2
Transmission Genetics

Student: _____ Section/Course: _____

Anticipation	Measured trait that usually fits within a bell-curve of readings
Autosomal	Tool that allows visualization of allele segregation in a cross
Backcross	A trait that always appears in the F1 of a Mendelian cross
Carrier	A trait that is not visible in the F1 of a Mendelian cross
Consanguineous	Used to visually identify inheritance patterns in a family
Consanguineous	Homozygous inheritance of these alleles will kill you
Deleterious	Individuals with different alleles of the same gene
Dominant	Individuals with identical alleles of the same gene
Haploid	A mutation that decreases chances of survival
Haploid	A group of genes affecting a single trait
Heterosis	An individual with a recessive allele
Heterozygous	Alternate to transmission genetics
Homozygous	Crossing a single trait
Lethal	Crossing three traits
Mating	Visible characteristic
Mendelian	Mendelian genetics aka
Monohybrid	The offspring of a cross
Paternity	Four-sided graphic Inheritance tool
Pedigree	The genetic makeup of Human gametes
Pedigree	Graphic chart showing familial inheritance
Phenotype	Having to do with non-sex chromosomes
Progeny	Mating indicated by double horizontal lines
Punnett	Testing a father using repeat-based markers
Punnett	This must be random in a population at equilibrium
Quantitative	These may interrupt a gene and cause lack of function
Quantitative	Common mating cause of rare autosomal recessive disease
Recessive	More severe symptoms at an earlier age in each generation
Transmission	Having half of the chromosomes required for a functional cell
Transposable	Crossing a desired parent into progeny for several generations
Trihybrid	Inheritance yielding a heterozygote with greater characteristics

Super-Matching 3
Population Genetics and People

Student: _____ Section/Course: _____

Population Genetics

Artificial	Cannot occur in a population at equilibrium
Conservation	Mutations not allowed in a critical gene
Domestication	Artificial selection of a plant or animal
Drift	Gene copies from a common ancestor
Evolution	Human-involved selection
Founder	"Origin of the ..."
Macro	Change over time
Migration	Rare allele in a population
Mutant	This "choice" determines survival
Natural	Creating a new separate population
Ortholog	Loss of genetic population variability
Paralog	Gene copies from within the same genome
Species	Evolution in which a new species is formed

People

Avery	Identified DNA as the hereditary material
Barr	First to isolate nucleic acids from cells
Chargaff	Identified important assumptions
Crick	Identified important assumptions
Darwin	Adenine equals thymine
Franklin	Father of Genetics
Hardy	Natural Selection
Macleod	Structure of DNA
McCarty	PCR Nobel prize
Mendel	Helical form of DNA
Miescher	Mostly inactivated X-chromosomes
Mullis	DNA as Griffiths transforming material
Stahl	Identified semi-conservative DNA replication
Weinberg	Identified DNA as Griffiths' transforming material

Super-Matching 4
Central Dogma

Student: _____ Section/Course: _____

Aneuploid	Mutation in codon that incorporates the same amino acid
Charged	A region of a transcript that will not be translated
Cytogenetics	Non-disjunction during development mitosis
Cytoplasm	Having an incorrect number of chromosomes
Deletion	Making a new type of molecule from RNA
Frames	Making a somewhat similar version of DNA
Genes	Nucleotides that perform a specific task
Introns	Main function of RNA polymerase
Mosaicism	Loss of a base pair in a sequence
Operon	Required for alternative splicing
RISC	Removes introns and potentially exons
Spliceosome	tRNA molecule with attached amino acid
Topoisomerase	siRNA regulation of mRNA occurs here
Transcription	There are six of these for each DNA sequence
Transcription	Works with microRNA to deactivate an mRNA
Translation	Related genes transcribed together in prokaryotes
UTR	Releases double stranded DNA in time for replication
Wobble	The study of the structure and function of chromosomes

How to Solve Scientific Method Abstract Worksheets

The scientific method is a series of steps that are followed to investigate possible solutions to a problem. An Investigator usually follows these basic guidelines:

1. Identify problem to be solved
2. Propose a testable hypothesis (solution)
3. Design a controlled experiment to test proposed solution
4. Perform the experiment, collecting data
5. Interpret the results, compare to expected results
6. Re-formulate hypothesis and re-test as necessary

These are all things that you do every day without thinking about it. Consider this: you may be hungry right now – perhaps you are thinking about eating a burrito or a cheeseburger. You have already identified the problem to be solved – your hunger. The next step is to propose a solution to the problem – it is obvious to you because you have been hungry before – eat food. How much food? Do you order two cheeseburgers or just one? As I hope that you now realize, you are already well into the scientific method. You have already identified the problem (hunger) and have hypothesized a solution (eating), which means the next step is to design a controlled experiment. Based on your past experience and on the level of hunger that you are experiencing, you can select the number of cheeseburgers that it will take to satisfy your hunger as your "controlled experiment". Let's say that you do not feel that hungry – so you order just one cheeseburger. All that is left is to perform the test. After consuming the food (step 4), you ask yourself a simple question "Am I still hungry?" if the answer is "yes", then you must reformulate your hypothesis (step 2 – now your hypothesis is that two cheeseburgers are required to satisfy your hunger), you eat the second cheeseburger and again ask yourself if you are hungry. Once you are no longer hungry, the number of cheeseburgers required to satisfy your hunger is the solution that you were seeking.

The above example is a very simple version of the scientific method. If this were an actual experiment, you would have a much harder time, since the problems are always in the details, and the details are what step three is about. Things like how much does each cheeseburger weigh? How much of this weight is meat and how much is bread or condiments? Lettuce? Pickles? Also, a large amount of variability will revolve around the subject – when was their last meal? How many calories was it? Are they male? Female? How old are they? What is their weight? All of these will affect the number of cheeseburgers that each person will need to eat before feeling full. Once you have these variables ironed out, then you will need to gain access to a test population – simply performing this test on one person will not answer anything – how many subjects do you think are needed? These are people, right? This means you must also have informed consent from each one of them. As you continue, you will begin to identify the weaknesses and strengths of each study, which will relate specifically to these six steps.

Your task is to label the steps of the scientific method in each abstract and answer a question about the study…..good luck!

Abstract 1   Student: _____   Section/Course: _____

Liu Y, Tang R, Zhao Y, Jiang X, Wang Y, Gu T. **Identification of key genes in atrial fibrillation using bioinformatics analysis**. BMC Cardiovasc Disord. 2020;20(1):363. Published 2020 Aug 10.

Abstract

Background

Atrial fibrillation (AF) is one of the most common arrhythmia, which brings huge burden to the individual and the society. However, the mechanism of AF is not clear. This paper aims at screening the key differentially expressed genes (DEGs) of atrial fibrillation and to construct enrichment analysis and protein-protein interaction (PPI) network analysis for these DEGs.

Indicate the Problem

Methods

The datasets were collected from the Gene Expression Omnibus database to extract data of left atrial appendage (LAA) RNA of patients with or without AF in GSE79768, GSE31821, GSE115574, GSE14975 and GSE41177. Batch normalization, screening of the differential genes and gene ontology analysis were finished by R software. Reactome analysis was used for pathway analysis. STRING platform was utilized for PPI network analysis. At last, we performed reverse transcription-quantitative polymerase chain reaction (RT-qPCR) to validate the expression of key genes in 20 sinus rhythm (SR) LAA tissues and 20 AF LAA tissues.

Indicate the Hypothesis

Indicate the Experiment

Results

A total of 106 DEGs were screened in the merged dataset. Among these DEGs, 74 genes were up-regulated and 32 genes down-regulated. DEGs were mostly enriched in extracellular matrix organization, protein activation cascade and extracellular structure organization. In PPI network, we identified SPP1, COL5A1 and VCAN as key genes which were associated with extracellular matrix. RT-qPCR showed the same expression trend of the three key genes as in our bioinformatics analysis. The expression levels of SPP1, COL5A1 and VCAN were increased in AF tissues compared to SR tissues ($P < 0.05$).

Indicate the data they analyzed

Indicate the Results

Conclusion

According to the analyses which were conducted by bioinformatics tools, genes related to extracellular matrix were involved in pathology of AF and may become the possible targets for the diagnosis and treatment of AF.

Indicate whether Successful

What central dogma enzyme is required for DEG production?

Abstract 2   Student: _____   Section/Course: _____

Wang M, Zhou Y, Zhang F, Fan Z, Bai X, Wang H. A novel MYH14 mutation in a Chinese family with autosomal dominant nonsyndromic hearing loss. BMC Med Genet. 2020;21(1):154. Published 2020 Jul 25.

Indicate the Problem

Abstract
Background
MYH14 gene mutations have been suggested to be associated with nonsyndromic/syndromic sensorineural hearing loss. It has been reported that mutations in MYH14 can result in autosomal dominant nonsyndromic deafness-4A (DFNA4).

Indicate the Hypothesis

Methods
In this study, we examined a four-generation Han Chinese family with nonsyndromic hearing loss. Targeted next-generation sequencing of deafness genes was employed to identify the pathogenic variant. Sanger sequencing and PCR-RFLP analysis were performed in affected members of this family and 200 normal controls to further confirm the mutation.

Indicate the Experiment

Results
Four members of this family were diagnosed as nonsyndromic bilateral sensorineural hearing loss with postlingual onset and progressive impairment. A novel missense variant, c.5417C > A (p.A1806D), in MYH14 in the tail domain of NMH II C was successfully identified as the pathogenic cause in three affected individuals. The family member II-5 was suggested to have noise-induced deafness.

Indicate the data they analyzed

Indicate the Results

Conclusion
In this study, a novel missense mutation, c.5417C > A (p.A1806D), in MYH14 that led to postlingual nonsyndromic autosomal dominant SNHL were identified. The findings broadened the phenotype spectrum of MYH14 and highlighted the combined application of gene capture and Sanger sequencing is an efficient approach to screen pathogenic variants associated with genetic diseases.

Indicate whether Successful?

Using the mutation at position 5417, complete this Punnett square showing a heterozygous affected individual and an unaffected mate and the genotypes of their possible progeny

	C	A

Abstract 3   Student: _____   Section/Course:_____

Tang J, Gao H, Liu Y, et al. **Network construction of aberrantly expressed miRNAs and their target mRNAs in ventricular myocardium with ischemia-reperfusion arrhythmias**. J Cardiothorac Surg. 2020;15(1):216. Published 2020 Aug 12.

Abstract

Background
Hypothermic ischemia-reperfusion arrhythmia remains the main factor affecting cardiac resuscitation under cardiopulmonary bypass. Existing research shows that certain miRNAs exhibit significantly different expressions and effects in arrhythmias, however, the effect of miRNAs on the progression of hypothermic ischemic–reperfusion arrhythmias (RA) and its potential mechanism remain to be further explored.

Methods
Sprague-Dawley (SD) rats were randomly divided into two groups (n = 8): a normal control group (Group C) and a hypothermic ischemia-reperfusion group (Group IR), which were used to establish a Langendorff isolated cardiac perfusion model. According to the arrhythmia scoring system, rats in group IR were divided into a high-risk group (IR-H) and a low-risk group (IR-L). miRNAs expression profiles of ventricular myocardium with global hypothermic ischemia–reperfusion and those of ventricular myocardium with hypothermic ischemia–RA were established through high-throughput sequencing. Furthermore, the aberrantly expressed miRNAs in myocardium with and without hypothermic ischemia–RA were screened and verified. The target genes of these aberrantly expressed miRNAs were predicted using RNAhybrid and MiRanda software. Based on Gene Ontology (GO) and the Kyoto Encyclopedia of Genes and Genomes (KEGG) databases, we determined the mRNA targets associated with these miRNAs and studied the miRNA–mRNA interaction during the cardiovascular disease progression. The aberrantly expressed miRNAs related to hypothermic ischemia–RA were validated by Real-time Quantitative polymerase chain reaction (RT-qPCR).

Results
Eight significantly aberrantly expressed miRNAs (rno-miR-122-5p, rno-miR-429, novel_miR-1, novel_miR-16, novel_miR-17, novel_miR-19, novel_miR-30, and novel_miR-43) were identified, among which six were up-regulated and two were down-regulated. Moreover, target genes and signaling pathways associated with these aberrantly expressed miRNAs were predicted and analyzed. The miRNA–mRNA interaction network graph showed that GJA1 gene was considered as the target of novel_miR-17.

Conclusions
Aberrantly expressed miRNAs were possibly associated with the formation mechanism of hypothermic ischemia–RA. Specific miRNAs, such as novel_miR-17 and rno-miR-429 are probably new potential targets for further functional studies of hypothermic ischemia–RA.

Use the Hardy-Weinberg Assumptions to discuss what could be done to continue this study?

Indicate the Problem

Indicate the Hypothesis

Indicate the Experiment

Indicate the data they analyzed

Indicate the Results

Indicate whether Successful?

Answers

Sequence Conversion 1
1. 5' - GCUCAUG - 3'
2. 5' - TACGAGT - 3'
3. 5' - UAGGUGU - 3'
4. 5' - GAAGCGA - 3'
5. 3' - AGCAGCA - 5'
6. 5' - UACCAAU - 3'
7. 5' - GAACGAT - 3'
8. 3' - ACGTTAG - 5'
9. 5' - UUGCAUC - 3'
10. 3' - AGTATCG - 5'

Sequence Conversion 2
1. 3' - CGGAGCT - 5'
2. 5' - TCTAGCG - 3'
3. 5' - CGAUACC - 3'
4. 3' - AAGCGTA - 5'
5. 5' - UAAGUAC - 3'
6. 3' - AGTGACG - 5'
7. 5' - MT - 3'
8. 5' - MSA - 3'
9. 5' - MRL - 3'
10. 5' - MCS - 3'

Sequence Conversion 3
1. B
2. 5' - UCUCGUG - 3'
3. 3' - AGCCGCA - 5'
4. 5' - GAACGCT - 3'
5. 5' - CUACAUC - 3'
6. 3' - CGGAGCT - 5'
7. 5' - CGACACC - 3'
8. 5' - UAAAUAC - 3'
9. 5' - MT - 3'
10. 5' - MWL - 3'

Sequence Conversion 4
1. A
2. 5' - CAAGAGT - 3'
3. 5' - GAAGCGA - 3'
4. 5' - CAACAAU - 3'
5. 3' - CGCCTAG - 5'
6. 5' - TCGAGGG - 3'
7. 3' - CAGCCTA - 5'
8. 3' - AGAGCCG - 5'
9. 5' - MSG - 3'
10. 5' - MH - 3'

Sequence Conversion 5
1. C
2. 3' - ACGACAG - 5'
3. 5' - GAUACUG - 3'
4. 5' - CTAATGT - 3'
5. 5' - UAGCAGU - 3'
6. 3' - ACCTGTA - 5'
7. 5' - GGATGCT - 3'
8. 5' - MRP - 3'
9. 5' - MSP - 3'
10. NO VALID START

Sequence Conversion 6
1. 5' - AAGGUGU - 3'
2. 3' - ACAAGCA - 5'
3. 5' - ACGTTAG - 3'
4. 5' - UUACAUC - 3'
5. 3' - AAGAGTA - 5'
6. 3' - AGTAACU - 5'
7. 5' - M STOP - 3'
8. 5' - MCA - 3'
9. 5' - MR STOP - 3'
10. 3' - TACTGGCCG - 5'

Mutation Annotation 1
1. C   "p" indicates polypeptide. "Thr" indicates the amino acid threonine.
2. C   complementary sequence to mutation
3. E   complementary sequence to mutation
4. 5' - TAT **C** AGGTAGC - 3'
5. 5' - LATRA **V** GSQGW - 3'
6. 1st bp of M codon "A" to "G"
7. 5' - ATCACATGAGTAGCAGT **A** AGTAGGATCAGTACAG - 3'
8. 5' - ATCACATGAGT **(A)** AGCAGTAAGTAGGATCAGTACAG - 3'
9. 5' - ATCAC ATG AGT CAT AGT AAG TAG GATCAGTACAG - 3'
           M   S   H   S   R   STOP
10. The third bp was deleted, causing a "T/U" to shift into the third codon position

Mutation Annotation 2
1. C;   a 1 bp deletion causes a frameshift in a gene encoding region
2. A or D are acceptable answers
3. B;   Frameshift will lead to very early termination
4. E;   B and C are not valid mutation notations (B "c" denotes sequence but shows amino acid; C "p" denotes polypeptide but shows DNA)
5. 5' - TATGAG **T** AGC - 3
6. 5' - LATRAMGSQG **C** - 3'
7. 3rd bp of W codon "G" to "C"

8. 5' - ATCACA **A** GAGTAGCAGTAAGTAGGATCAGTACAG - 3'
9. 5' - ATCAC ATG AGT CAT AGT AAG TAT TAA CAGTACAG - 3'
          M   S   H   S   K   Y STOP
10. The first bp of the codon was a "G" modified to a "T/U" resulting in a termination codon

Probability of Random Match 1
1   This is basic math with 4 to the sixth power; 4; 16; 64; 256; 1024; 4096; The odds are 1 in 4096 or 1/4096.
2   This is basic math with 4 to the fourth power; 4; 16; 64; 256; The odds are 1 in 256 or 1/256.
3   This is basic math with 4 to the fifth power; 4; 16; 64; 256; 1,024; The odds are 1 in 1,024 or 1/1,024.
4   D   This has a 6bp recognition site, or about once every 4,000 bp of random DNA
5   A   This has a 4bp recognition site, or about once every 250 bp of random DNA
6   5' - GGATCC - 3'
7   About 8 bp or every 65,000 bp (15.3 sites on average in 1 Mbp)
8   About 3 times; Calculator based answer 3,000,000,000/1,073,741,824 = ~3 times
9   Both C and E are good answers (higher annealing temperature increases specificity)
10 XhoI recognizes a 6 base restriction site, so about 25; calculator based 100,000/4,096 = 24.41

Probability of Random Match 2
1   This is basic math with 4 to the seventh power; 4; 16; 64; 256; 1024; 4096;16,384 The odds are 1 in 16,384
2   This is basic math with 4 to the third power; 4; 16; 64; The odds are 1 in 64 or 1/64.
3   This is basic math with 4 to the eigth power = 65,536 or 1/65,536
4   D   This has a 6bp recognition site, or about once every 4,000 bp of random DNA
5   B   This has a 6bp recognition site, or about once every 4,000 bp of random DNA
6   5' - CCCGGG - 3'
7   About 8 bp or every 65,000 bp - likely to cut 1 to 2 times
8   About 3,000 times; Calculator based answer 3,000,000,000/1,048,576 = 2,861 times
9   Both A and B are good answers
10 About 250; BSP13I is a 6 base cutter.

Probability of Random Match 3
1   First, convert to the probability of each base A or T = .3; G or C = .2; now do the math
    .3 x .3 x .3 x .2 x .2 x .3 = 0.000324; 1/.000324 = 1 in 3,086 bp
2   First, convert to the probability of each base A or T = .2; G or C = .3; now do the math…
    .3 x .3 x .3 x .3 = 0.0081; 1/.0081 = 1 in 123 bp
3   Tryptophan (W) only has one codon, thus 1 of 64 (1/64) possible codons will result in W. First, identify how many of the 64 possible codons encode the specific amino acid. P = 4/64 ; Q = 2/64; W = 1/64;
    reduced fractions 1/16 x 1/32 x 1/64 = 1/32,768
4   B
5   B
6   What is the sequence recognized by HaeII? (A/G) GCGC (T/C) The (A/G) indicates that either A OR G will work, or T OR C will work.
7   How many restriction sites will HaeII find in a 100,000 bp fragment of DNA? ½ x ¼ x ¼ x ¼ x ¼ x ½ = 1,024 or about 100 sites
8   How many times would you expect to find a 16 bp primer sequence in Humans (3 Bbp DNA) 4^{16} = 4.29 billion - or about one time in 3 Bbp;
9   E or C are the best answers
10 About 25; MroI is a 6 base cutter.

Cross Probability 1
1   25%
2   0%
3   25%
4   50%
5   33%
6   1/8
7   1/32
8   1/16
9   Chromosome 21 non-disjunction - Down syndrome.
10 Autosomal recessive disease. Parents are related and likely share recessive disease alleles

Cross Probability 2
1. 50%
2. 0%
3. 100%
4. 33%
5. 100%
6. 1/8
7. 1/32
8. 1/16
9. 1/8
10. 50%; the SNP information is irrelevant.

Cross Probability 3
1. 50%
2. 50%
3. 25%
4. 50%
5. 25%
6. 25%
7. 50%
8. 0% males cannot be carriers
9. 1/32
10. Both parents unhealthy, siblings unhealthy; likely rare homozygous dominant disease

Pedigree 1
1. Parents of II-5 (I-1 and I-2); Parents of III-2 and III-4 (II-1 and II-4) each received copy from I-1 or I-2.
2. 50%
3. V-1, V-3, V-4, V-5, V-6, III-3, III-4, II-1, II-4
4. IV-1, III-1, III-2, III-6, II-3; I-1 or I-2 is a carrier
5. Generation V is already married; must be at least 20 years old, add 20 years minimum for each generation; at latest 1920 but more likely before 1900.

Pedigree 2
1. III-1; The proband is the person who brings the family under study and since tIII-1 is the only one showing symptoms of the disease, the would be the proband
2. II-1 is II-2s first husband and is relevant due to their child; II-3 is II-2s second husband, who is likewise relevant due to their two children
3. II-1 and II-2 MUST be carriers
4. Either I-1 or I-2; possibly II-4 or II-6; Possibly children of II-4, III-4, III-5, III-6.
5. First, determine who MUST be a carrier; In this case, III-3 and III-4 are obvious, but so are II-2 and II-5. *Test them? sure, why not*...Second, who would need to know? IV-1, III-1, III-2 and III-5 *should be tested* because they are still young enough to potentially have children. Testing generation II might be informative, but they are likely in their 40s to 50s, so are unlikely to have more children.
6. Either by directly sequencing any samples that may have been preserved, testing either side of their extended families descendants. In the end it would not be a useful endeavor, since it would not change the carrier or disease status of the current generations.

Pedigree 3
1. II-4 as this is the most likely shared ancestor to III-3 and III-6; An argument could also be made that II-3 and II-5 have the shared ancestor I-2, who may have passed the allele to their sons.
2. 50%
3. Most likely II-2 as no other living relatives appear to be affected
4. Since III-4 and III-5 have a shared ancestry, II-3 and II-5 and either I-1 or I-2 were also likely affected.
5. 75%; Since they are both heterozygotes for the dominant allele (ex: Dd x Dd). *Autosomal dominant homozygotes are actually quite rare.*

Pedigree 4
1. Daughters of II-2 (III-1 and III-2) are carriers; Daughter of II-4 (III-4) is a carrier; Mother of II-2 and II-4 (I-2) is a carrier
2. Daughters of II-2 and II-3 are carriers (III-1 and III-3)
3. V-5 MIGHT be a carrier; III-5 is a carrier
4. Sons of affected I-2 are affected (II-2, II-3, II-5, II-6); III-4 might be affected (if II-4 is affected)

Pedigree 5

1. IV-1 daughter of affected male (III-3); II-3 mother of affected male III-3; Either II-4 OR II-5 parents of III-4; This one is tricky - because II-3 is NOT part of this family, it is possible that II-4 could be the source of the dominant condition. If II-5 is the source of III-4, then I-2 is affected. Related mating is not relevant.
2. When a shared ancestry makes transmission of a disease through generations, this is the route to take; II-1 and II-3 have affected daughters; Because II-3 is a male, this means that I-2 is most likely source (males cannot pass X chromosomes on to their sons)
3. Shared ancestry with affected II-4 means II-2 (parent of III-1) and I-2 must have been affected.

Pedigree 6

1. Derive I-1 16/27 from II-2 and II-6; Add 16 to II-1 from III-1 – because II-2 cannot be 27/16 (must get one copy from each parent); Now add 17 to II-2 from III-2; Derive 19/24 for II-5 by using only those sizes that are not in the parents of II-4. This leaves 27/31 for II-4 derived from remaining III-3 and III-4 children
2. Derive III-2, III-3, III-4 as 310 from homozygous parent II-4; Derive II-1, II-3 and II-5 as 330 from homozygous parent I-2; Derive II-1 325 from child III-1, then derive I-1 325 from II-1; Derive II-3 315 from child III-4, then derive I-1 315 from II-3; Derive II-6 320 from child III-5 (Parents I-1 and I-2 do not have 320, must come from II-6).
3. Derive II-2 and II-3 C from III-4; Add C to II-3 (known homozygous), then add C to III-3 from II-3; Derive II-1 AT from III-1 and III-2 (these alleles cannot be from II-2); Derive II-5 C from III-6; II-2 and II-5 only share a C, so this must be the homozygous allele - CC to I-1, A to I-2

Pedigree 7

1. T
2. F — No affected parent for III-6
3. F — II-3 and III-3 would be affected
4. F — I-1 would have to be affected and is required to pass affected allele to II-3
5. T

Forensics 1

TM40	B	
TM41	E	"15/18" means that the tested alleles have 15 repeats in one and 18 repeats in the other
TM42	C	Although there *could* be 245 and 259 repeats, this is unlikely; most SSRs are picked to have a 100-300 bp length for simplified detection.
TM7	B	Because the parents of the victim are homozygous, they must 120/120 and 125/125; only suspect 6 has the required alleles to be a sibling.

Forensics 2

1. E — Just because the suspect is homozygous does not mean the parents are as well
2. B
3. C
4. D; All can be related to the victim since only two alleles are given - remember that each parent only provides one allele to a child; without knowing the parents' alleles any relationship cannot be determined.

Forensics 3

1. Shown at right
2. 130 (6 alleles in the population) or 145 (4 alleles in the population).
3. 115 appears to be the rarest band size with only one allele in the population
4. 6/18 = 0.333 or 33.3%
5. 1/18 = 0.055 or 5.5%
6. If the DNA is directly linked to the criminal act, none of the suspects committed the crime.

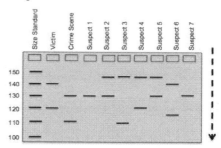

Forensics 4

2. 130 with 6 of 18 alleles (counting the crime scene sample, which is not among the suspects)
3. 110, 115 or 150 are the likely the rarest in the population, with only one copy in this small sample.
4. 6 of 18 is 33.3%
5. 1 of 18 is 5.5%
6. The suspects included in this sample are highly unlikely to be the perpetrator of the crime

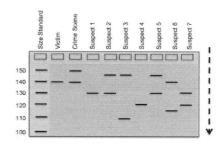

Paternity 1
1. Alleles unique to **father 1** in child 1 are D7S820 216, VWA160, etc…
2. Alleles unique to **father 3** in child 2 are TPOX 227, D3S1358 112, etc…
3. Alleles unique to **father 1** in child 3 are TPOX 220, FGA 300, etc…
4. 216/237
5. 136/165
6. 122/160
7. Between the three children there are six alleles at each molecular marker locus, but only four alleles between the parents. If there are five unique alleles at any locus, there must be a second father. In the example below the five parental alleles for D3S1358 indicate a second father. It gets even easier with more than three children - there is still a four allele limit….

example:

Marker	Child 1	Child 2	Child 3	Parental alleles
TPOX	216/220	227/237	220/237	216, 220 227, 237
D3S1358	99/147	99/112	106/134	99, 147, 112, 106, 134

Paternity 2
1. Alleles unique to **father 1** in child 1 are D7S820 216, VWA160, etc…
2. Alleles unique to **father 3** in child 2 are TPOX 227, D3S1358 112, etc…
3. Alleles unique to **father 1** in child 3 are TPOX 220, FGA 300, etc…
4. 284/320
5. 99/147
6. 300/? – unable to determine the 2nd allele
7. A maternity test may be required for children switched at birth, kidnapping or adoption at a young age; Additional answers are possible.

Paternity 3
1. You suspect that your sister is adopted. Assuming you have a sample of her DNA, which combination of individuals' DNA could you test to determine if she is your sister?
   - A Yes. This is a straight paternity test and will confirm that your sister is your fathers' daughter. Your mothers' DNA is not needed (this could also be a *maternity* test).
   - B Yes. This is a straight maternity test and will confirm that your sister is your mothers' daughter. Your grandparents' DNA is not needed.
   - C Yes. This is a straight maternity test and will confirm that your sister is your mothers' daughter. Your aunt's DNA is not needed.
   - D Yes. This is *still* a straight paternity test and will confirm that your sister is your fathers' daughter. Your paternal grandparents are your fathers' parents, thus they have all alleles that your father would have; Instead of two possible paternal alleles, there are now up to *four*, one of which must be possessed by your sister for each marker.
   - E Yes. This is *still* a straight maternity test and will confirm that your sister is your mothers' daughter. Your maternal grandparents are your mothers' parents, thus they have all alleles that your mother would have; Instead of two possible maternal alleles, there are now up to *four*, one of which must be possessed by your sister for each marker.
   - F Maybe. If they are your brothers, there would only be four possible allele sizes at each molecular marker. Your sister would then have to match these; It is highly likely that you could determine whether she is your sister using you and your siblings' DNA.
   - G Yes. This is *still* a straight maternity/paternity test and will confirm that she is your sister. Your grandparents have all alleles that your mother and father would have; Instead of two possible maternal alleles, there are now up to *eight*, one of which must be possessed by your sister for each marker.

Paternity 4

1.

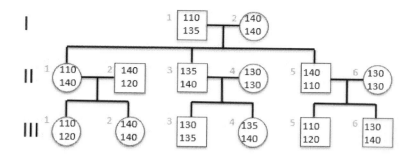

2. Using a Punnett square, the remaining combinations are 110/140 and 120/140
3. Using a Punnett square, all possible combinations are already present in their children (110/140 and 135/140)
4. III-4 cannot be the daughter of II-4 (does not have a 130 allele) and III-5 cannot be the son of II-6 (does not have a 130 allele).
5. There are five alleles in this pedigree. 110, 120, 130, 135, 140;
6. All of the alleles in question five can be passed on to the next generation

Alleles in a Population 1
1. D   start with square root of affected; q = .4, p = .6; $p^2+2pq+q^2$; $.6^2 + 2(.6)(.4) + .4^2$ = 36 unaffected homozygous + 48 heterozygous carriers + 16 affected
2. A   start with square root of affected; q = .6, p = .4; $p^2+2pq+q^2$; $.4^2 + 2(.4)(.6) + .6^2$ = 16 unaffected homozygous + 48 heterozygous carriers + 36 affected
3. D   divide the numbers given by ten to make the calculation easier....100 people, 4 affected; q=.2, p = 0.8
4. C   divide the numbers given by ten to make the calculation easier....100 people, 4 affected; q=0.2, p=0.8.
5. D   ....100 people, 4 affected; q=.2, p = 0.8
6. A   ....20 people, 5 affected; q=.5; p = 0.5; (0.5 x 0.5 = 25% are affected, 50% heterozygous and 25% homozygous unaffected) This is a Punnett square.
7. B;   ....20 people, 5 affected; q=.5; p = 0.5; (0.5 x 0.5 = 25% are affected, 50% heterozygous and 25% homozygous unaffected) This is a Punnett square.

Alleles in a Population 2
1. 48   Start with square root of affected; q = .4 thus p = .6; $p^2+2pq+q^2$; $.6^2 + 2(.6)(.4) + .4^2$ = 36 homozygous unaffected + 48 heterozygous carriers + 16 affected
2. 64   Because this disease is dominant, the p^2 and $2pq$ represent *affected* people. First, find q, which is 1.0 - affected (36) which = .64; the square root of .64 is .8 and this is q (and p is .2). Now solve the equation; $p^2+2pq+q^2$; $.2^2 + 2(.2)(.8) + .8^2$ = 4 homozygous affected + 32 heterozygous affected + 64 homozygous unaffected
3. 32   Because this disease is dominant, the p^2 and $2pq$ represent *affected* people. First, find q, which is 1.0 - affected (36) which = .64; the square root of .64 is .8 and this is q (and p is .2). Now solve the equation; $p^2+2pq+q^2$; $.2^2 + 2(.2)(.8) + .8^2$ = 4 homozygous affected + 32 heterozygous affected + 64 homozygous unaffected
4. 42   Start with square root of affected; q = .3 thus p = .7; $p^2+2pq+q^2$; $.7^2 + 2(.7)(.3) + .3^2$ = 49 homozygous unaffected + 42 heterozygous carriers + 9 homozygous affected
5. 1   Start with square root of affected; q = .1 thus p = .9; $p^2+2pq+q^2$; $.9^2 + 2(.9)(.1) + .1^2$ = 81 homozygous unaffected + 18 heterozygous carriers + 1 homozygous affected
6. 18   Start with square root of affected; q = .1 thus p = .9; $p^2+2pq+q^2$; $.9^2 + 2(.9)(.1) + .1^2$ = 81 homozygous unaffected + 18 heterozygous carriers + 1 homozygous affected
7. 86.5   Start with square root of affected; q = 0.005 or 0.07) thus p = .93; $p^2+2pq+q^2$; $.93^2 + 2(.93)(.07) + .07^2$ = 86.5 homozygous unaffected + 13 heterozygous carriers + 0.5 homozygous affected
8. 96.38%   Start with the square root of affected; (q = $\sqrt{0.000333}$ or 0.01825) thus p = .98175; $p^2+2pq+q^2$; $.98175^2 + 2(0.98175)(0.01825) + 0.01825^2$ = 96.38% homozygous unaffected + 3.58% heterozygous carriers + 0.000333% homozygous affected
9. 99.97%   Start with the square root of affected; (q = $\sqrt{0.000333}$ or 0.01825) thus p = .98175; $p^2+2pq+q^2$; $.98175^2 + 2(0.98175)(0.01825) + 0.01825^2$ = 96.38% homozygous unaffected + 3.58% heterozygous carriers + 0.000333% homozygous affected

Alleles in a Population 3

1. 36 — Start with square root of affected; q = .4 thus p = .6; $p^2+2pq+q^2$; $.6^2 + 2(.6)(.4) + .4^2$ = 36 homozygous unaffected + 48 heterozygous carriers + 16 affected

2. 84 — Start with square root of affected; q = .4 thus p = .6; $p^2+2pq+q^2$; $.6^2 + 2(.6)(.4) + .4^2$ = 36 homozygous unaffected + 48 heterozygous carriers + 16 affected

3. 4 — Because this disease is dominant, the p^2 and 2pq represent *affected* people. First, find q, which is 1.0 - affected (36) which = .64; the square root of .64 is .8 and this is q (and p is .2). Now solve the equation; $p^2+2pq+q^2$; $.2^2 + 2(.2)(.8) + .8^2$ = 4 homozygous affected + 32 heterozygous affected + 64 homozygous unaffected

4. 9 — Start with square root of affected; q = .3 thus p = .7; $p^2+2pq+q^2$; $.7^2 + 2(.7)(.3) + .3^2$ = 49 homozygous unaffected + 42 heterozygous carriers + 9 homozygous affected

5. 49 — Start with square root of affected; q = .3 thus p = .7; $p^2+2pq+q^2$; $.7^2 + 2(.7)(.3) + .3^2$ = 49 homozygous unaffected + 42 heterozygous carriers + 9 homozygous affected

6. 81 — Start with square root of affected; q = .1 thus p = .9; $p^2+2pq+q^2$; $.9^2 + 2(.9)(.1) + .1^2$ = 81 homozygous unaffected + 18 heterozygous carriers + 1 homozygous affected

7. 13 — Start with square root of affected; q = 0.005 or 0.07) thus p = .93; $p^2+2pq+q^2$; $.93^2 + 2(.93)(.07) + .07^2$ = 86.5 homozygous unaffected + 13 heterozygous carriers + 0.5 homozygous affected

8. 99.5 — Start with square root of affected; q = 0.005 or 0.07) thus p = .93; $p^2+2pq+q^2$; $.93^2 + 2(.93)(.07) + .07^2$ = 86.5 homozygous unaffected + 13 heterozygous carriers + 0.5 homozygous affected

9. 3.58% — Start with the square root of affected; (q = $\sqrt{0.000333}$ or 0.01825) thus p = .98175; $p^2+2pq+q^2$; $.98175^2 + 2(0.98175)(0.01825) + 0.01825^2$ = 96.38% homozygous unaffected + 3.58% heterozygous carriers + 0.000333% homozygous affected

Crossword Puzzle 1

Crossword Puzzle 2

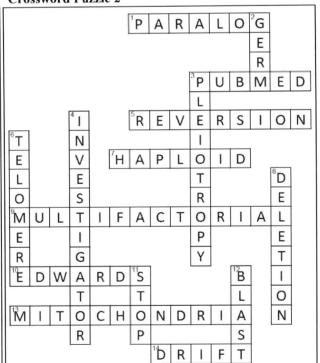

Crossword Puzzle 3

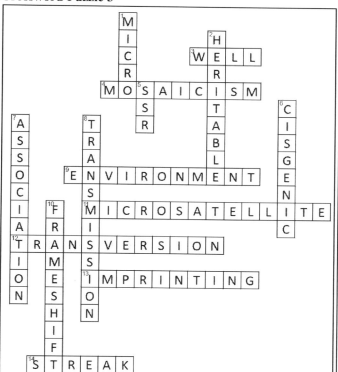

Crossword Puzzle 4

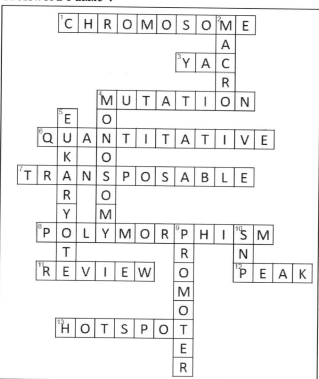

Lab-Based Exercise 1
1. Institution specific
2. Institution specific
3. Institution specific
4. Institution specific
5. T
6. A
7. C
8. Blowout, eject aspirate and dispense (BEAD)
9. 873 ul
10. 3 ul
11. D   equals 2.15 ml or 0.00215 L; E is a distance.

Lab-Based Exercise 2
1. Institution specific
2. Institution specific
3. Institution specific
4. F
5. F; DNA is not consumed in the PCR reaction
6. F; 100o C
7. T
8. T
9. T
10. T
11. F
12. Water, DNA polymerase, buffer, free nucleotides, DNA template, primers, MgCl$_2$
13. B
14. The samples would evaporate due to the heated lid being below 100° C

Lab-Based Exercise 3
1. Institution specific
2. Institution specific
3. Institution specific
4. E   This sequence has a 60% G/C content (the highest of all possible answers)
5. D   This has a 6bp recognition site, or about once every 4,000 bp of random DNA
6. A   This has a 4bp recognition site, or about once every 250 bp of random DNA
7. C   Use the rule of 3 000s for every 5 base pairs
8. D   Use the rule of 3 000s for every 5 base pairs
9. E   Use the rule of 3 000s for every 5 base pairs

Lab-Based Exercise 4
1. C   This sequence has a 30% G/C content (the lowest of all possible answers)
2. B   One amino acid is encoded by each codon
3. A   One amino acid is encoded by each codon, each codon is 3 bp 3 x 930 = 2,790
4. C   One amino acid is encoded by each codon
5. B   ITS database is used extensively to identify bacterial unknowns
6. A
7. B
8. E

Super Matching 1

Agar	Growth media
Agarose	Electrophoresis matrix
Annealing	Primers attach to DNA in PCR
Band	Similar-sized fragments on a gel
Blot	Remove excess liquid
Centrifuge	Separates samples by spinning
Chamber	The device that holds running buffer for electrophoresis
Colony	Multiple copies of a single bacteria
Comb	Creates agarose wells for sample loading
Denaturation	The separation of DNA strands using heat
Dispense	Expel liquid from a pipettor
Enzyme	Catalyzes a reaction
Evaporation	Prevented by a heated lid in PCR
Hybridization	DNA base pair matching
Incubate	Grow bacteria under specific conditions
Ladder	Size standard for electrophoresis
PCR	Copy DNA using temperature cycling
Peak	The top of a fragment in capillary detection
Pellet	Combined sample after spinning
Petri	A dish best served to bacteria
Pipette	Device used to transfer small amounts of liquid
Primer	Fragment of DNA used to start PCR
Restriction	To cleave/cut a molecule
Sanger	Oldest still viable sequencing method
Sterile	Free from bacteria or other living organisms
Streak	Spreading your sample across growth media
Tare	Reset a scale
Transilluminator	Allows detection of DNA in a gel
Well	Cavity in an agarose gel for sample loading

Super Matching 2

Anticipation	More severe symptoms at an earlier age in each generation
Autosomal	Having to do with non-sex chromosomes
Backcross	Repeated crossing of a desired parent into progeny for several generations
Carrier	An individual with a recessive allele
Consanguineous	Mating indicated by double horizontal lines
Consanguineous	Very common mating cause of rare autosomal recessive disease
Deleterious	A mutation that decreases chances of survival
Dominant	A trait that always appears in the F1 of a Mendelian cross
Haploid	Having half of the chromosomes required for a functional cell
Haploid	The genetic makeup of Human gametes
Heterosis	This inheritance type yields a heterozygote with greater characteristics
Heterozygous	Individuals with different alleles of the same gene
Homozygous	Individuals with identical alleles of the same gene
Lethal	Homozygous inheritance of these alleles will kill you
Mating	This must be random in a population at equilibrium
Mendelian	Alternate to transmission genetics
Monohybrid	Crossing a single trait
Paternity	Testing a father using repeat-based markers
Pedigree	Graphic chart showing familial inheritance
Pedigree	Used to visually identify inheritance patterns in a family
Phenotype	Visible characteristic
Progeny	The offspring of a cross
Punnett	A tool that allows visualization of the allele segregation in a cross
Punnett	Four-sided graphic Inheritance tool
Quantitative	A group of genes affecting a single trait
Quantitative	A measured trait that usually fits within a bell-curve of readings
Recessive	A trait that is not visible in the F1 of a Mendelian cross
Transmission	Mendelian genetics aka
Transposable	These elements may interrupt a gene and cause lack of function

Trihybrid   Crossing three traits

Super Matching 3
Population Genetics

Artificial	Human-involved selection
Conservation	Mutations not allowed in a critical gene
Domestication	Artificial selection of a plant or animal
Drift	Loss of genetic population variability
Evolution	Change over time
Founder	Creating a new separate population
Macro	Evolution in which a new species is formed
Migration	Cannot occur in a population at equilibrium
Mutant	Rare allele in a population
Natural	This "choice" determines survival
Ortholog	Gene copies from a common ancestor
Paralog	Gene copies from within the same genome
Species	"Origin of the ..."

People

Avery	Identified DNA as Griffiths transforming material
Barr	Mostly inactivated X-chromosomes
Chargaff	Discovered equal A and G DNA composition
Crick	Discovered structure of DNA
Darwin	Proposed Natural Selection
Franklin	Identified Helical form of DNA
Hardy	Discovered important assumptions
Macleod	Identified DNA as Griffiths transforming material
McCarty	Identified DNA as the hereditary material
Mendel	Father of Genetics
Miescher	First to isolate nucleic acids from cells
Mullis	PCR Nobel prize
Stahl	Identified semi-conservative DNA replication
Weinberg	Discovered important assumptions

Super Matching 4

Aneuploid	Having an incorrect number of chromosomes
Charged	tRNA molecule with attached amino acid
Cytogenetics	The study of the structure and function of chromosomes
Cytoplasm	siRNA regulation of mRNA occurs here
Deletion	Loss of a base pair in a sequence
Frames	There are six of these for each DNA sequence
Genes	Nucleotides that perform a specific task
Introns	Required for alternative splicing
Mosaicism	Non-disjunction during development mitosis
Operon	Related genes transcribed together in prokaryotes
RISC	Works with microRNA to deactivate an mRNA
Spliceosome	Removes introns and potentially exons
Topoisomerase	Releases double stranded DNA in time for replication
Transcription	Main function of RNA polymerase
Transcription	Making a somewhat similar version of DNA
Translation	Making a new type of molecule from RNA
UTR	A region of a transcript that will not be translated
Wobble	Mutation in codon that incorporates the same amino acid

Abstract 1

Modified From:
Liu Y, Tang R, Zhao Y, Jiang X, Wang Y, Gu T. **Identification of key genes in atrial fibrillation using bioinformatics analysis**. BMC Cardiovasc Disord. 2020;20(1):363. Published 2020 Aug 10.

Indicate the Problem
Atrial fibrillation (AF) is one of the most common arrhythmia, which brings huge burden to the individual and the society. However, the mechanism of AF is not clear.

Indicate the Hypothesis
This paper aims at screening the **key differentially expressed genes (DEGs)** of atrial fibrillation and to construct enrichment analysis and protein-protein interaction (PPI) network analysis for these DEGs.

Indicate the Experiment
The datasets were collected from the Gene Expression Omnibus database to extract data of left atrial appendage (LAA) **RNA of patients with or without AF** in GSE79768, GSE31821, GSE115574, GSE14975 and GSE41177. Batch normalization, screening of the differential genes and gene ontology analysis were finished by R software. Reactome analysis was used for pathway analysis. STRING platform was utilized for PPI network analysis. At last, we performed reverse transcription-quantitative polymerase chain reaction (RT-qPCR) to validate the expression of key genes in 20 sinus rhythm (SR) LAA tissues and 20 AF LAA tissues.

Indicate the Data they analyzed
A total of 106 DEGs were screened in the merged dataset. Among these DEGs, **74 genes were up-regulated and 32 genes down-regulated**.

Indicate the Results
DEGs were mostly enriched in extracellular matrix organization, protein activation cascade and extracellular structure organization. In PPI network, we identified SPP1, COL5A1 and VCAN as key genes which were associated with extracellular matrix. RT-qPCR showed the same expression trend of the three key genes as in our bioinformatics analysis. The expression levels of SPP1, COL5A1 and VCAN were increased in AF tissues compared to SR tissues ($P < 0.05$).

Indicate whether Successful
genes related to extracellular matrix were involved in pathology of AF and may become the possible targets for the diagnosis and treatment of AF.

What central dogma enzyme is required for DEG production? **RNA polymerase**

Abstract 2

Modified From:
Wang M, Zhou Y, Zhang F, Fan Z, Bai X, Wang H. A novel MYH14 mutation in a Chinese family with autosomal dominant nonsyndromic hearing loss. BMC Med Genet. 2020;21(1):154. Published 2020 Jul 25.

Indicate the Problem
MYH14 gene mutations have been suggested to be associated with nonsyndromic/syndromic sensorineural hearing loss. It has been reported that mutations in MYH14 can result in autosomal dominant nonsyndromic deafness-4A (DFNA4).

Indicate the Hypothesis
Targeted next-generation sequencing of deafness genes was employed to identify the pathogenic variant.

Indicate the Experiment
In this study, we examined a four-generation Han Chinese family with nonsyndromic hearing loss.
Sanger sequencing and PCR-RFLP analysis were performed in affected members of this family and 200 normal controls to further confirm the mutation.

Indicate the Results
Four members of this family were diagnosed as nonsyndromic bilateral sensorineural hearing loss with postlingual onset and progressive impairment.

Indicate the Data they analyzed
A novel missense variant, c.5417C > A (p.A1806D), in MYH14 in the tail domain of NMH II C was successfully identified as the pathogenic cause in three affected individuals. The family member II-5 was suggested to have noise-induced deafness.

Indicate whether Successful?
In this study, a novel missense mutation, c.5417C > A (p.A1806D), in MYH14 that led to postlingual nonsyndromic autosomal dominant SNHL were identified. The findings broadened the phenotype spectrum of MYH14 and highlighted the combined application of gene capture and Sanger sequencing is an efficient approach to screen pathogenic variants associated with genetic diseases.

Using the mutation at position 5417, complete this Punnett square showing a heterozygous affected individual and an unaffected mate.
The annotation c.5417C > A indicates that the "C" base at position 5417 has been mutated to an "A", which causes the condition.

	C	A
C	C/C	C/A
C	C/C	C/A

Abstract 3

Modified from:
Tang J, Gao H, Liu Y, et al. **Network construction of aberrantly expressed miRNAs and their target mRNAs in ventricular myocardium with ischemia-reperfusion arrhythmias**. J Cardiothorac Surg. 2020;15(1):216. Published 2020 Aug 12.

Indicate the Problem
Hypothermic ischemia-reperfusion arrhythmia remains the main factor affecting cardiac resuscitation under cardiopulmonary bypass.

Indicate the Hypothesis
Existing research shows that certain miRNAs exhibit significantly different expressions and effects in arrhythmias, however, the effect of miRNAs on the progression of hypothermic ischemic–reperfusion arrhythmias (RA) and its potential mechanism remain to be further explored.

Indicate the Experiment
Sprague-Dawley (SD) rats were randomly divided into two groups (n = 8): a normal control group (Group C) and a hypothermic ischemia-reperfusion group (Group IR), which were used to establish a Langendorff isolated cardiac perfusion model. According to the arrhythmia scoring system, rats in group IR were divided into a high-risk group (IR-H) and a low-risk group (IR-L). miRNAs expression profiles of ventricular myocardium with global hypothermic ischemia–reperfusion and those of ventricular myocardium with hypothermic ischemia–RA were established through high-throughput sequencing. Furthermore, the aberrantly expressed miRNAs in myocardium with and without hypothermic ischemia–RA were screened and verified.

Indicate the data they analyzed
The target genes of these aberrantly expressed miRNAs were predicted using RNAhybrid and MiRanda software. Based on Gene Ontology (GO) and the Kyoto Encyclopedia of Genes and Genomes (KEGG) databases, we determined the mRNA targets associated with these miRNAs and studied the miRNA–mRNA interaction during the cardiovascular disease progression. The aberrantly expressed miRNAs related to hypothermic ischemia–RA were validated by Real-time Quantitative polymerase chain reaction (RT-qPCR).

Indicate the Results
Eight significantly aberrantly expressed miRNAs (rno-miR-122-5p, rno-miR-429, novel_miR-1, novel_miR-16, novel_miR-17, novel_miR-19, novel_miR-30, and novel_miR-43) were identified, among which six were up-regulated and two were down-regulated. Moreover, target genes and signaling pathways associated with these aberrantly expressed miRNAs were predicted and analyzed. The miRNA–mRNA interaction network graph showed that GJA1 gene was considered as the target of novel_miR-17.

Indicate whether Successful?
Aberrantly expressed miRNAs were possibly associated with the formation mechanism of hypothermic ischemia–RA.

Use the Hardy-Weinberg Assumptions to discuss what could be done to continue this study?
This question requires the student to form an opinion about the presented study and the answers will vary.
Here are my quick thoughts, which are *not* a key....:-)
How could you use the Hardy-Weinberg assumptions to plan future research directions? The answer is almost always the same...although the study was performed on rats, the GJA1 gene is located on chromosome 6q22 in Humans, so the first questions are whether the miR-17 sequence is produced in humans, if not, this is a dead end. If the miR-17 miRNA is produced in humans, then changes in sequence of the miR-17, or the GJA1 mRNA (mutation) could be be associated with Humans suffering Hypothermic ischemia-reperfusion arrhythmia. Of course, once we start talking about mutations, then the rest of the H-W assumptions come in to play - are there particular regions where a mutation is present (migration) or where this procedure is more/less successful? Is there an effect on the production of offspring (Natural Selection) - probably not, as cardic problems are more prevalent in older individuals.

Printed in Great Britain
by Amazon